How to Teach
for
METACOGNITIVE
REFLECTION

—◆—

by

Robin Fogarty

IRI/Skylight Publishing, Inc.

Palatine, Illinois

The Mindful School: How to Teach for Metacognitive Reflection
First Printing

Published by IRI/Skylight Publishing, Inc.
200 East Wood Street, Suite 274
Palatine, IL 60067
800-348-4474, 708-991-6300
FAX 708-991-6420

Creative Director: Robin Fogarty
Editors: Julia E. Noblitt, Erica Pochis
Writer: Liesl Banks-Stiegman
Type Compositor: Donna Ramirez
Book Designer: Bruce Leckie
Cover Designer and Illustrator: David Stockman
Production Coordinator: Amy Behrens

Library of Congress Catalog Card Number 93-80673

Printed in the United States of America.

ISBN 0-932935-49-4

0755-2-94

Dedication

For Brian, whose gift is insight into oneself . . .

TABLE OF
CONTENTS

Introduction . . . vii

SECTION I

PLANNING STRATEGIES ... 1

1. *Stem Statements* [Thoughtful Lead-Ins] . . . 5
2. *Inking Your Thinking* [Learning Logs] . . .13
3. *Film Footage* [Visualization] . . . 21
4. *Fat and Skinny Questions* [Higher-Order Questions] . . . 29
5. *Roll the Dice* [Predicting] . . . 37
6. *Pie in the Face* [Making Inferences] . . . 45
7. *The Goal Post* [Goal Setting] . . . 55
8. *A Road Map* [Strategic Planning] . . . 63
9. *Seesaw Thinking* ["What-If" Problem Solving] . . . 71
10. *Prime the Pump* [KWL] . . . 79

SECTION II

MONITORING STRATEGIES ... 87

1. *Talk to Yourself* [Think Aloud] . . . 93
2. *Soup Cans* [Labeling Behaviors] . . .103
3. *Alarm Clock* [Recovery Strategies] . . . 111
4. *Instant Replay* [Tape Recordings] . . . 121
5. *Post-it Note* [Memoing] . . . 131
6. *Mental Menus* [Tracking] . . . 139
7. *Cue Cards* [Prompting] . . . 149
8. *Two-Way Talk* [Conferencing] . . . 157
9. *Transfer Talk* [Bridging] . . . 167
10. *The Microscope* [Recorded Observations] . . . 177

TABLE OF CONTENTS

SECTION III
EVALUATING STRATEGIES ... 187

1. *Thumbs Up/Thumbs Down* [PMI] . . . 191
2. *Choose Your Spot* [The Human Graph] . . . 201
3. *Mrs. Potter's Questions* [Evaluating] . . . 211
4. *A Revolving Door* [The Portfolio Registry] . . . 221
5. *Connecting Elephants* [How Can I Use This?] . . . 231
6. *The Big Idea* [Generalizing] . . . 241
7. *Checkmate!* [Self-Administered Checklists] . . . 251
8. *What? So What? Now What?* [Student-Led Conferences] . . . 261
9. *Storytime!* [Anecdotes] . . . 271
10. *Double-Talk* [Double-Entry Journals] . . . 281

Bibliography . . . 303
Index . . . 309

METACOGNITION

What's it all about, Alfie?

An intellect is someone whose mind watches itself.
—Albert Camus

Metacognition—thinking about thinking; but exactly what does that mean? Metacognition is not even in the dictionary. It sounds pretty esoteric, doesn't it? And if asked to define metacognition or describe it, you might feel somewhat inadequate. It's like trying to explain atomic fusion to a five-year-old; you can conceptualize it in your mind, but you don't know how to tell someone else—in simple language—what it is.

In the early '80s when the thinking skills movement was in its infancy, to use the word metacognition in a teacher workshop was risky; people actually became hostile. One time a veteran teacher stood up, red in the face and demanded, "Why do you have to use words like these? Can't you speak English?"

To take some of the mystery (and hostility) out of the word, there are several examples of metacognition that may make it easier to grasp.

A WORKING DEFINITION

Think about a time when you were reading and suddenly you got to the bottom of a page of text and a little voice inside your head said, "I don't know what I just read." With this awareness of knowing what you *don't* know, you employ a recovery strategy and you read the last sentences; you scan the page of paragraphs looking for key words; you reread the entire page. Whatever you do, you capture the meaning and go on. This awareness—knowing what you know and what you don't know is called metacognition:

> A reader who reads and reads and reads and doesn't know that he doesn't is not using metacognition. The key to metacognitive behavior is this self-awareness of one's own thinking and learning. "Once you know, you can't not know" and, in fact, you can then adjust accordingly. So metacognition is awareness and control over your own thinking behavior.

> To have awareness and control over your own thinking one may plan metacognitively, monitor progress metacognitively, or evaluate metacognitively. Thus, the three areas, planning, monitoring, and evaluating provide the appropriate framework for self-reflection.

PLANNING

Let me give a more specific example of metacognition in the planning stages that might clarify the concept. As a teacher, you plan your lessons prior to class; you take into consideration myriad variables including time, complexity, prior knowledge, student population, etc. This planning phase, the time when you predict, prepare, and plan your day is a metacognitive time for you.

During this preparation time, it's almost as if you are standing *outside* the situation—looking in; you are imagining the actual lesson and the reaction(s) of the class to your plans; you are in essence removed from the action. This is metacognitive planning.

MONITORING

Once you begin the actual teaching of the lesson, you move into the cognitive realm. You enter into the context of the subject matter content and execute your lesson plan. You are inputting information for student understanding. However, often in the midst of the teaching act, teachers move out of that cognitive arena and into the metacognitive. Let me illustrate.

Halfway into your explanation of photosynthesis, you notice signs of confusion. One student is rifling through the pages of his science book looking for the part in the text that explains photosynthesis. Another student is doodling a diagram of the process in her notebook, but you can see it is incomplete. Several hands are raised and other students have a glazed look in their eyes.

Noticing all this, in an instantaneous glance up from the blackboard, you immediately shift gears and ask students to turn to their partner and ask a question they have about the process of photosynthesis. After a few minutes—after the partners have tried to answer each other's question, you ask for some sharing so you can clarify the concepts for everyone.

This monitoring of the students' reactions and the resulting adjustment to the instructional input is metacognitive in nature. Whenever we watch student behaviors and log the information for "minor adjustments or repairs"—we act metacognitively—beyond the cognitive. It's as if we do a "freeze frame" on the teaching in the classroom; an instant replay format—we take a second look at what's going on. This is metacognition.

EVALUATING

If you're still confused—or feeling vague about metacognition, let me give you a further example of metacognitive reflection as evaluation.

Think back to your childhood—about something you memorized years ago; a poem, a song, a theorem—maybe even the multiplication tables. It can be anything.

"Four score, and seven years ago." "ABCDEFG . . . ," "Twas the night before Christmas and all through the house," "Yours is not to reason why—just invert and multiply." Next, recite that piece from memory, right now. Say it aloud to yourself.

Now, think about how you learned that piece so many years ago that to this very day you can recall it—instantly and accurately. Think about the strategies used to learn this so that you can recite it by "rote memory." This evaluative thinking—assessing what you know, how, and why you know it—this thinking is metacognitive; thinking about how you learn and being able to generalize those skills and strategies for transfer and use into diverse situations—that's metacognitive reflection.

WHAT DO THE EXPERTS SAY?

In 1979, John Flavell used the term metacognition to describe "active monitoring and consequent regulation and orchestration of [cognitive] processes, usually in the service of some concrete goal or objective." He went on to identify four elements in metacognitive ability: metacognitive knowledge, experiences, goals, and strategies.

Early work done by Feuerstein (1978) in this area shed light on the emerging concept of metacognition. Through a series of tasks developed over a period of time, Feuerstein's work in cognitive mediation guides students through self-monitoring activities that lead to reflective behavior and transfer. Feuerstein's ground-breaking work in this area and in-depth longitudinal studies in the field, provide substantive cognitive theory on which others have built. In fact, Feuerstein's landmark study demonstrates the modifiability of cognitive behavior and changes the view of intelligence as an unchanging entity to a capacity that grows not only in developmentally appropriate ways with age, but also through deliberate interventions or "mediated learning experience."

According to Brown's research (1980) in reading, metacognition is what good readers do when they read the plan, monitor, and evaluate throughout the process. Brown & Palincsar (1982) believe that we can teach those metacognitive strategies to all children as a way to unlock the reading process for them.

On the other hand, Costa defines metacognition as our ability to know what we know and what we don't know. It is our ability to plan a strategy for producing what information is needed, to be conscious of our own steps and strategies during the art of problem solving, and to reflect on and evaluate the productivity of our own thinking.

Costa goes on to say, [when] you hear yourself talking to yourself . . . if you [are] having an inner dialogue inside your brain and if you evaluate your own decision-making/problem-solving processes—you [are] experiencing metacognition.

Costa summarizes the research on metacognition as Planning, Monitoring, and Evaluating:

> Planning a strategy before embarking on a course of action helps us track the steps. It facilitates making judgments; assessing readiness for different activities; and monitoring our interpretations, perceptions, decisions, and behaviors. An example of this is what superior teachers do daily; develop a teaching strategy for a lesson, keep that strategy in mind throughout the instruction, then reflect upon the strategy to evaluate its effectiveness in producing the desired student outcomes.

Self-Monitoring

Rigney (1980) identified the following self-monitoring skills as necessary for successful performance on intellectual tasks: keeping one's place in a long sequence of operations, knowing that a subgoal has been obtained, and detecting errors and recovering from those errors.

In addition, (1) *looking ahead* includes: learning the structure of a sequence of operations, identifying areas where errors are likely, choosing a strategy that will reduce the possibility of error and provide easy recovery, and identifying the kinds of feedback that will be available and evaluating the usefulness of this feedback, while (2) *looking back* includes: detecting errors previously made, keeping a history of what has been done and what should come next, and assessing the reasonableness of the immediate outcome.

Yet, some believe that not everyone is metacognitive. Whimbey and Whimbey (1976) state that all adults metacognate, while Sternberg and Wagner (1982) say some children have virtually no idea what they are doing when they perform a task and are often unable to explain their strategies for solving problems.

HOW TO TEACH—NOT DIRECT—BUT INFUSE

Others focus their writing on how to teach for metacognition. If we wish to develop intelligent behavior as a significant outcome of education, instructional strategies purposefully intended to develop children's metacognitive abilities must be infused into our teaching methods, staff development, and supervisory processes (Costa, 1981). Interestingly, *direct* instruction in metacognition may *not* be beneficial. When strategies of problem solving are imposed rather than generated by the students themselves, their performance may be impaired. Conversely, when students experience the need for problem-solving strategies, induce their own, discuss them, and practice them to the degree that they become spontaneous and unconscious, their metacognition seems to improve (Sternberg and Wagner, 1982). The trick, therefore, is to teach metacognitive skills without creating an even greater burden on students' ability to attend.

STRATEGIES FOR ENHANCING METACOGNITION

Costa suggests specific strategies:

> *Planning Strategy.* *Prior* to any learning activity, teachers should point out strategies and steps for attacking problems, rules to remember, and directions to follow. *During* the activity, teachers can invite students to share their progress, thought process, and perceptions of their own behav-

ior. *After* the learning activity, teachers can invite students to evaluate how well the rules were obeyed.

Generating Questions. Regardless of the subject area, it is useful for students to pose study questions for themselves prior to and during their reading of textual material.

Choosing Consciously. Teachers can promote metacognition by helping students explore the consequences of their choices and decisions prior to and during the act of deciding.

Evaluating with Multiple Criteria. Teachers can enhance metacognition by causing students to reflect upon and categorize their actions according to two or more sets of evaluative criteria. An example would be to invite students to distinguish what was done that was helpful or hindering; what they liked or didn't like; and what were pluses and minuses of the activity.

Taking Credit. Teachers may cause students to identify what they have done well and invite them to seek feedback from their peers. The teacher might ask, "What have you done that you're proud of?" and "How would you like to be recognized for doing that?" (Name on the board, hug, pat on the back, handshake, applause from the group, and so on.) Students will become more conscious of their own behavior and apply a set of internal criteria for those behaviors that they consider good.

Outlawing "I Can't." Students should be asked to identify what information is required, what materials are needed, or what skills are lacking in their ability to perform the desired behavior. This helps students identify the boundaries between what they know and what they need to know.

Paraphrasing or Reflecting Back Students' Ideas. Some examples of paraphrasing, building upon, extending, and using students' ideas might be to say: "What you're telling me is . . ." "It seems you're saying . . ." "I think I hear. . . ."

Labeling Students' Behaviors.   When teachers place labels on students' cognitive processes, students become conscious of their own actions: "What I see you doing is making out a plan of action for…"; "What you are doing is called an experiment"; "You're being very helpful to Mark by sharing your paints. That's an example of cooperation."

Clarifying Students' Terminology.   Students often use hollow, vague, and nonspecific terminology. For example, in making value judgments, students might say, "It's not fair," "He's too strict," "It's no good." Teachers need to clarify these values: What's too strict? What would be more fair?

Role Playing and Simulations.   Role playing can promote metacognition because when students assume the roles of other persons, they consciously maintain the attributes and characteristics of that person. Dramatization serves as a hypothesis or prediction of how that person would react in a certain situation. Taking on another role contributes to the reduction of ego-centered perceptions.

Journal Keeping.   Writing and illustrating a personal log or a diary throughout an experience causes students to synthesize thoughts and actions and to translate them to symbolic form. The record also provides an opportunity to revisit initial perceptions, to compare changes in those perceptions with the addition of more data, to chart the processes of strategic thinking and decision making, to identify the blind alleys and pathways taken, and to recall the successes and the tragedies of experimentation. (A variation on writing journals is making video and/or audio tape recordings of actions and performances.)

Modeling.   Of all the instructional strategies, modeling the model is by far the most effective. The adage, actions speak louder than words proves to be true. If students see teachers model behaviors such as delineating a plan and justifying a choice, students are more likely to exhibit those same behaviors.

Beyer (1987) elaborates on a cueing technique to prompt metacognition. Questions Beyer suggests to foster metacognitive behavior are: What am I doing? Why am I doing it? What other way can I do it? How does it work? Can I do it again or another way? How could I help someone else do it?

Current research by Swartz and Perkins (1989) refines the concept of metacognition beyond the accepted, generalized definition of awareness of and control over one's own mind and thinking. They distinguish four levels of metacognitive thought: tacit use, aware use, strategic use, and reflective use.

Tacit Use	without thinking about it
Aware Use	aware that and when
Strategic Use	conscious strategies
Reflective Use	reflects before, during, and after

Tacit use is using a skill or strategy without consciously thinking about the fact that a particular skill or strategy is being employed. For example, little children go into a temper tantrum to get what they want. They automatically revert to this strategy when they're not getting their way. They know that the behavior works. Yet, they are not consciously aware of what they're doing or why they're doing it.

By contrast, aware use of a skill or strategy signals another level of metacognitive behavior. When a child is aware of the reaction a certain behavior gets, the child begins to sense some control over his environment. To follow the temper tantrum example, a child who is becoming aware of how this behavior affects his desired outcome instantly stops crying at the slightest intervention of any sort; being picked up, cooing, a dangled toy, etc. It's almost as if we can see the suspended thinking of the child as he processes what is going on—what results he has gotten from his actions. He is becoming aware of a cause-effect relationship.

In turn, the third level of metacognition delineated by Swartz and Perkins is labeled strategic use. It involves deliberate, conscious, mapped use of that skill or strategy. At this stage, the child in our example consciously maps out a plan. He now knows that if he cries and stomps his feet he will not only get the attention he wants, but he will most likely get *what* he wants because he's tried this strategy before and he knows it works. Therefore, he employs his skills and strategies consciously with a strategic plan in mind.

Finally, the fourth level of metacognition signals the most sophisticated use incorporating reflection and self-evaluation. A child displaying this reflective stage of metacognition evaluates a number of viable strategies to get what he wants: throw a temper tantrum, pout, whimper, tease or joke. After reflecting on his choices and evaluating his chances with each, he selects the one he feels is best.

In summary, in the last twenty years of cognitive research, the literature presents an evolving picture of metacognition as a critical component of the intellect. Only when one becomes aware of his or her own behavior, can he or she begin to be self-regulatory about that behavior. Only when one can step back "beyond the cognitive moment" and plan, monitor, and evaluate can he or she begin to understand and change.

WHY BOTHER TO TEACH FOR METACOGNITION?

As the literature on metacognition expands and the concept of metacognitive reflection unfolds, the practical implication for the classroom becomes more clear. In fact, at first glance, there are three obvious reasons to include metacognitive classroom interactions. The first reason is related to the constructivists' view of learning, while the second reason is connected to the prevalent line of cooperative, collaborative models of classroom interactions. And, finally, the third reason has to do with fostering transfer of learning to novel situations.

More specifically, constructivists view learning as the process individuals experience as they take in new information and make sense of that information. By making meaning, they are acquiring knowledge. However, individuals who construct knowledge and are aware of the gaps in their understanding of that knowledge are actively using both their cognitive and their metacognitive strategies. In their awareness of what they know and what they don't know, they take the first step in remedying the deficit areas. Thus, both cognition and metacognition are necessary elements in constructing meaning.

Also, in today's classroom the use of cooperative learning and small group work is considered a cornerstone of the active learning models. As students work together, they have opportunities to articulate their thinking and in the process, internalize learning. As students put ideas into their own words, they learn differently; they learn more substantially. However, the increased use of interactive models dictates an equally increased use of reflective tools; personal reactions in which students go inside their own heads and think about their learning. That personal reflection is embedded in the metacognitive processing of the classroom in which students look back and look over their progress.

Still a third call for metacognitive reflection comes with the ultimate purpose of learning . . . to transfer and use that learning in other places. To foster meaningful application and transfer of learning, student reflection is key. Again, metacognitive strategies provide the necessary format to promote learning not just for a test, but for a lifetime—not just for recall, but for lifelong logic and reasoning.

METACOGNITION AND THE TEACHER

As teachers and educators—as architects of the intellect, we can foster and guide the metacognitive behavior of our learners. Using the staid and true model of the thoughtful classroom that suggests that we teach for, of, with, and about thinking, an emerging idea begins to make sense of quality instruction.

Teaching **FOR** Thoughtfulness (Satisfactory)	Teaching **OF** Thoughtfulness (Good)
Teaching **WITH** Thoughtfulness (Excellent)	Teaching **ABOUT** Thoughtfulness (Superior)

Teaching FOR Thoughtfulness

In the classroom, the *satisfactory* teacher sets a warm and caring climate for students to feel good about themselves and to build their self-confidence and faith in their abilities. This teacher is concerned with the affective as well as the cognitive development of students.

> In her fifth grade classroom, Mrs. Roderick talks to her students about the strategy of "wait-time." She explains that after she asks a question, no one is to answer—they are to take three to ten seconds to wait and to think. By utilizing this strategy of "silence," she sets a safe climate and high expectations for all students to think before they answer.

Teaching OF Thoughtfulness

The *good* teacher goes beyond setting the climate *for* a thoughtful classroom. This teacher addresses the microskills of thinking and explicitly teaches both critical and creative thinking in a direct instruction model to ensure that students know the skills and have the tools for lifelong learning.

> For example, this teacher incorporates the microskill of predicting by asking students to generate synonyms for predicting: forecasting, anticipating, etc. She probes for examples of when they use predicting: weather, moods of parents, reaction of friends, etc., and infuses predicting strategies into the subject matter context: predict reasonable answers in math; predict outcomes of experiments in science; predict story endings in literature, etc.

Teaching WITH Thoughtfulness

Paralleling this profile of the good teacher is the *excellent* teacher who not only creates a warm and caring climate *for* thinking and employs a direct instruction in the skills *of* thinking, but also incorporates the strategies of a truly interactive classroom to teach *with* thinking. Cooperative learning strategies become an integral part of the learning environment as students become actively involved in their learning experiences. Graphic organizers are used extensively in all group work so student thinking is both visible and audible as they cooperatively solve problems and complete assigned tasks.

For example, using graphic organizers such as webs and mind maps to depict their thinking about a science unit and using cooperative learning groups to jigsaw a social studies chapter in the text are typical instructional activities that foster active learning and intense student involvement.

Teaching ABOUT Thoughtfulness

Finally, in this ideal scenario, the *superior* teacher goes "beyond the cognitive and into the metacognitive." The superior teacher knows that setting the climate for thinking and teaching explicit skills through cooperative learning must be accompanied by reflective discussion strategies to make meaning of the learning. By giving deliberate attention to not only what they're doing, students learn to think about the how and why of what they're doing. This reflection allows them to process their thinking and behavior and in turn foster transfer and application of their learnings.

For example, after a learning activity, the teacher asks students to complete a stem for their log entry: After working with fractions today, I'm wondering.... Or the teacher may require students to reflect on their strategies in the cooperative groups: "Talk about what you did well today as a group and what you can improve upon...."

FOUR ELEMENTS: IN SUMMARY

By including the four distinct areas of teaching for, of, with, and about thinking—the skillful teacher teaches not only for the moment, but for the long run. The superior teacher naturally causes students to be aware of their own learning and to be strategic and reflective about that learning. This thoughtful student reflection, in turn, fosters creative application and transfer of ideas as students bridge learning into their everyday lives.

THE METACOGNITIVE MIRRORS

Once we understand the concept of metacognition and the value it has in deep understanding for learning, we are ready to explore the various tools and strategies that foster metacognition. In the broadest sense, these techniques fall into three distinct categories as suggested by Costa and others. The three arenas are planning, monitoring, and evaluating.

Let me create an image of these three processes that may illuminate the ideas and at the same time provide an ongoing metaphor for the ideas in the book. The concept of metacognition is like a mirror, because both illuminate flaws as well as positive attributes, change with time, and provide not only first glimpses but second looks.

To carry the mirror metaphor even further, there are various kinds of mirrors that seem respectively appropriate to the various types of *metacognitive reflection.* The mirrors for reflective planning are the full-length, three-way mirrors found in the dressing rooms of large department stores. These triple lenses provide full exposure to all angles—quite a necessary view as one lays out plans, trying to anticipate the many facets of an idea.

Yet, the mirrors for *reflective monitoring* are the rear view and side view mirrors found on cars, trucks, and vans, allowing clear sightings as one proceeds along a chosen path. These personally positioned mirrors provide the needed perspectives to guide progress, signal the need for adjustments, and allow for margins of error in each particular situation.

Finally, the magnifying mirror of a compact seems most appropriate for *reflective evaluation*. This hand-held mirror enlarges the selected image for careful scrutiny and close, in fact, microscopic evaluation. With this larger-than-life view, reflections are easily inspected for subtle flaws or positive characteristics.

And, just as each mirror is used discretely for different purposes, so too are the metacognitive tools used specifically for different purposes: to look ahead and plan; to look over and monitor; or to look back and evaluate.

ABOUT THE BOOK

Three major sections provide the categorical labels for fostering reflective metacognition in student work:

Section I: Planning Techniques

Section II: Monitoring Mechanisms

Section III: Evaluating Tools

Within each section, ten specific strategies are developed for immediate use in the classroom. Among these strategies are stem statements, mental problem-solving, think-aloud techniques, double-entry journals, and artifact evaluation tools.

While many of the strategies will be familiar to the reader, the purpose of this work is to identify, label, and illustrate the use of the instructional methodologies as metacognitive tools that help students reflect on their learning. By embedding the ideas in the contextual framework of metacognitive tools, teachers can more easily inventory reflective strategies they are already using and refine those. In addition, they will be introduced to new ones, also.

SECTION
I

PLANNING
Strategies for Students to Use

We must ask where we are and wither we are tending.
—Abraham Lincoln

To revisit the mirror metaphor, the full-length, dressing room mirror with its three-way panels provides quite a comprehensive image. This full reflection, from several divergent angles, is exactly the scope that is needed in the early planning stages of metacognitive behavior.

The planning stage provides an opportunity to fully anticipate the strengths and weaknesses of an idea or proposition. It is in the preliminary phase of an endeavor that careful scrutiny is possible because the project is still under construction. It is in this planning period that adjustments and changes are most easily made, because nothing is actually set in place yet.

Therefore, the three-way mirror allows that rare look at the back side of an idea or that stark profile that often eludes the cursory look that occurs when one is in the heat of the action.

Reflective planning lays precious groundwork for later refinement. The more completely the real image is exposed early in the process, the more likely successful implementation will follow.

In this planning section, ten metacognitive strategies are illuminated for immediate use. These ideas include stem statements, learning logs, a visualization strategy, fat and skinny questions, predicting, inferencing, goal setting, strategic planning, mental problem solving, and the KWL. Each idea is discussed briefly, examples illustrate the practical use of the strategy, and an application opportunity structured into the section allows readers to try out the idea in a personally relevant example.

Remember, the best laid plans of mice and men often go astray—so plan with care and reflect on that plan for its strengths and flaws.

PLANNING 10 STRATEGIES

1. *Stem Statements* [Thoughtful Lead-Ins] . . . 5

2. *Inking Your Thinking* [Learning Logs] . . . 13

3. *Film Footage* [Visualization] . . . 21

4. *Fat and Skinny Questions* [Higher-Order Questions] . . . 29

5. *Roll the Dice* [Predicting] . . . 37

6. *Pie in the Face* [Making Inferences] . . . 45

7. *The Goal Post* [Goal Setting] . . . 55

8. *A Road Map* [Strategic Planning] . . . 63

9. *Seesaw Thinking* ["What-If" Problem Solving] . . . 71

10. *Prime the Pump* [KWL] . . . 79

STRATEGY 1

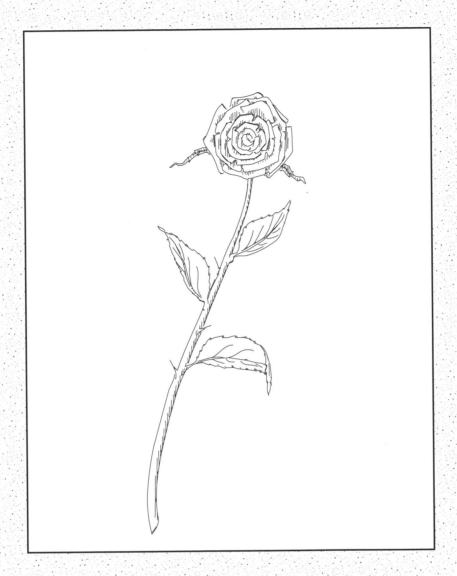

Stem Statements

[THOUGHTFUL LEAD-INS]

THOUGHTFUL LEAD-INS

What

Stem statements such as these can give the students thought prompts to stimulate personal responses . . . orally, in written form, or perhaps in artistic designs. They are referred to as stem statements because, much like the stem of a flower, the stem statement represents only part of the entire picture. And, just as with a flower, the students' thinking grows from the stem; it blossoms with elaboration that is relevant and helpful for student understanding.

Stem statements guide thinking in a number of directions. Stem statements stir the pot with prior knowledge and past experiences. Often stem statements are given by the teacher as facilitator, but eventually,

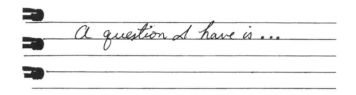

as students become more sophisticated in their use of metacognitive strategies, they generate their own stems. This is appropriate as students can then select stems that are personally relevant.

Why

The research on metacognition in the area of reading strongly suggests that tapping into prior knowledge benefits the students. Prompting thinking about what students already know sets the stage for new information. In *Becoming a Nation of Readers*, Anderson et al. postulate that reading is constructive as well as strategic (1984).

In the past, reading instruction has emphasized "post reading" strategies, with scant attention to "prereading" or "during-the-reading" intervention. The instructional program is represented thusly:

THOUGHTFUL LEAD-INS

**TRADITIONAL READING
INTERVENTION ACTIVITIES**

Emphasis was on the comprehension activities following the reading, with minor attention to the title and background connections. Students were inundated with follow-up work to check for understanding. Questions were posed that evaluated how much they had retained from the selection.

Anderson et al., however, suggest a model that reflects their constructivist view of learning. Their approach might resemble this model:

**CONSTRUCTIVIST READING
INTERVENTION ACTIVITIES**

In this model, ample cues are given prior to the reading for students to think about in order to make relevant connections to the upcoming text. Students are consistently expected to think ahead and to anticipate happenings as they create a mind set for the reading. Of course, the implication is that with this alert state, they will be more "ready" to understand and comprehend.

This constructivist theory of learning provides the rationale for the stem statement strategy. It seems appropriate and valid as a prompting technique to key students into prior knowledge and past experience, getting ready to connect the known to the unknown.

THOUGHTFUL LEAD-INS

How

To use stem statements, the teacher or facilitator may simply put the stem on the board or overhead transparency. Students can then react to it by writing in their notebooks or journals. Or, they may respond orally to a partner and share their ideas.

Another effective method to use is the wraparound strategy. In this strategy, students are placed in small, cooperative groups. After the teacher presents the stem statement, students first think about it themselves and jot down an individual response on scratch paper. Then, after all have a moment to reflect, they respond orally to the group by using a response-in-turn or the wraparound strategy. This is similar to the round robin idea. However, when using the wraparound, students are instructed *not* to judge the responses, but to accept all ideas in a rapid-fire progression. For example, the "I wonder . . ." stem speaks three very different thoughts about water. "I wonder why some water is salty?" "I wonder why water falls from the sky?" "I wonder why water is wet?" Each response is simply acknowledged as the next speaker begins.

When

To make the stem statement strategy effective as a metacognitive planning tool for students, it is, of course, necessary to use it before the learning episode. An especially powerful example is the high school biology teacher who uses stem statements immediately at the start of the day to get the students ready for the lesson at hand. This works quite readily as a way of reviewing the work from the day before and then moving students toward the new material. "A connection I made yesterday was. . . ."

Also, the stem statement is appropriate to introduce a whole unit of study as well as just one day's lesson. This, too, acts as a prompt for student thinking as they enter into the new unit. It develops a mind set for focused learning. One illustration is the stem: "I predict that this unit on living things will include plants and animals from the past and present. I hope that it includes dinosaurs."

One Idea

 Before beginning a unit or reading information from a text on a topic, ask your students to complete responses to stems or lead-ins you provide. Once they have responded by recording their thoughts, ask them to share these with a partner. Hold a brief class discussion about their stems to pique their interest in the topic and tap into their prior knowledge. Remind the students that many of their questions and concerns may be answered in the reading or during the unit or study.

Here are examples of completed stems from elementary students about to study the environment and endangered species.

SAMPLE STEMS

One thing I know about this topic is . . . *that whales are endangered animals.*

I wonder . . . *what other animals are endangered? This reminds me of the time we went to the aquarium and the tour guide said that many animals are on the endangered species list.*

A word I've heard before is . . . *extinction.*

A question I have is . . . *What can people do to help save the animals?*

My Idea

Jot down one idea for this metacognitive tool.

_____

_____

_____

_____

_____

_____

_____

_____

_____

_____

_____

_____

My Reflection

What I Did

Log your use of the idea. Explain what you actually did, giving some details but mostly just the "big idea."

_____

_____

_____

_____

_____

_____

_____

_____

_____

_____

_____

_____

_____

What I Think

Reflect on the activity. What are the pluses and minuses? What other thoughts do you have?

_____

_____

_____

_____

_____

_____

_____

_____

_____

_____

_____

_____

_____

Afterthoughts

STRATEGY 2

Inking Your Thinking

[LEARNING LOGS]

LEARNING LOGS

hat Learning logs are simple tools that can be used with students as pre-learning prompts. First, it is important to understand what is meant by a learning log. To clarify the concept of learning logs, it might help to discuss what they are not. They are not personal journals or daily diaries in which students write their feelings and concerns of the moment; and they are not class notebooks in which students take down the comments of the teacher to complement the discussion provided in the text. Learning logs are written entries that relate directly to the learning at hand. Used as pre-learning prompts or cues, statements or questions written in the logs are often mediated by teachers as they direct students to think about the lesson or reading they are about to do. For example, students may be asked to jot down a thought from yesterday's class to help them recall what was under discussion and to help them connect to the day's topic. The biology teacher asks students to note in their individual logs, one puzzling question from the assigned homework reading. Students are then expected to scan the chapter and find a section that was unclear or troubling.

Learning logs may be separate booklets used specifically and solely for logging student thinking. Or they may be a separate section of another notebook that is designated for log entries. The key to learning logs is that the student's writing is directly tied to the learning of the moment. In this case, the log entry is a precursor to the learning episode as the student captures ideas prior to the learning. The student thinks about "bias"—a concept she is studying in relation to the media. In her entry, she connects to her own personal biases.

LEARNING LOGS

A pioneer in the use of learning logs as metacognitive tools for students is Peter Elbow. In his two classic texts on student writing, *Writing Without Teachers* (1973) and *Writing With Power* (1981), Elbow outlines the use of logs for students as part of his self-directed learning model. In the examples, he has students write about their writing: how they feel about writing that day, their goals for the day, and other comments of interest or concerns they may have. Logging ideas before actually beginning to write stirs up prior knowledge and helps bridge the previous day's writing with the ideas brewing for today. Elbow finds the log a viable tool for students as they accept more and more responsibility for their own learning. Further explanations of learning logs are elaborated in *Patterns for Thinking: Patterns for Transfer,* by Fogarty and Bellanca (1987). In this book, the use of the log extends beyond the planning stage and into logging before, during, and after the learning.

How

The procedure for using learning logs begins with the introduction of the tool to students and frequent, but appropriate use throughout the semester or year. To introduce the learning log to students, if possible show them logs that students have produced in previous years. This is always inspiring to students. If, however, this is your first time using them, simply begin by folding over a few sheets of paper and stapling them to resemble a small booklet. Then give students a simple writing assignment for the day using lead-in statements that require them to reflect on the lesson they are about to begin. Sample starters might be: I predict . . ., An idea I have about . . ., I wonder . . ., A question I have is . . ., What if . . ., This compares to . . ., A picture I have of this is . . . .

In addition to the simple lead-in is the mediated log entry in which the teacher directs the student by giving guidelines for the beginning, the middle, and the end of the entry. For example, a mediated entry about a math lesson might look like one of these:

LEARNING LOGS

The homework problem that puzzles me is . . .

The way I will solve my problem is to . . .

This strategy might be called . . .

The important thing to remember about this strategy is . . .

**When** Although learning logs are appropriate to use throughout the day, this metacognitive strategy is particularly useful just before starting the day's lesson. Its purpose is to jump-start the thinking about the topic, concept, or skill that will be the focus of the impending lesson. In addition, the mediated log entry allows students to reflect on their personal approach to the task. This guided reflection helps students to recognize and to then generalize about the strategies that they use. By taking a few moments for students to reflect on their thinking and their ways of working through something, the chances of putting those ideas into long-term memory for future strategic use is more likely to occur. When learning is anchored in the minds of the learners, when learning is fully internalized, it is more available to the learner for future application and use. The possibility of meaningful transfer is greatly increased.

Ironically, just as in our approach to reading comprehension, the learning log is most often used *after* the fact. Just as we quiz students on their comprehension *after* the reading rather than stirring up prior knowledge before they read, the learning log is highly effective as a prelearning strategy. It gets students ready to learn. Instead of the "Ready! Fire! Aim!" approach, it is the "Ready! Aim! Fire!" model.

One Idea

 In addition to assigning math homework problems for practice, also require students to complete a brief mediated log entry before they try the problem solving. This technique can be especially useful for both teachers and students. Middle school students trying to grasp the concepts of algebra can use these logs to think about their learning and convey problems that they are having to the teacher. Teachers can read the learning logs when collecting student homework for a quick assessment of how students are approaching problem solving and what strategies they select first.

Start by using these stems in the learning logs.

- The homework problem that puzzles me is . . .

- The way I will solve this problem is to . . .

- I'm choosing this strategy because . . .

Prior to beginning the next lesson, ask students to discuss their learning logs in small groups. Ask them to find out if others are using a similar strategy or if someone can help them to better understand a strategy. Next, share the highlights of the group discussions with the whole class. Perhaps some areas need further explanation and practice. Allow students to work in groups to complete additional practice problems. Ask them to record their thoughts on the day's lesson in their learning logs.

My Idea

Jot down one idea for this metacognitive tool.

_____

_____

_____

_____

_____

_____

_____

_____

_____

_____

_____

_____

_____

_____

_____

_____

My Reflection

What I Did

Log your use of the idea. Explain what you actually did, giving some details but mostly just the "big idea."

_____

_____

_____

_____

_____

_____

_____

_____

_____

_____

_____

_____

_____

What I Think

Reflect on the activity. What are the pluses and minuses? What other thoughts do you have?

_____

_____

_____

_____

_____

_____

_____

_____

_____

_____

_____

_____

_____

Afterthoughts

STRATEGY 3

Film Footage

[VISUALIZATION]

VISUALIZATION

What

Visualization is the act of mentally imaging, or picturing in the mind, an idea or situation—imagining or seeing the unknown with the proverbial "mind's eye." To visualize or to perceive something is to capture a mental image. For example, in reading, we create mental pictures of the characters and the setting. Often, if we see a film, after having read the book, we invariably say, "The book was better," because the visualized images are personally constructed in the readers' minds, while the film images are created by the director, actors, etc. To visualize is to see; to make visible the otherwise invisible. Visualization is a specialized form of perception that can be "trained" with practice. Visualization is what Joe Wayman (1980) calls, "the other side of reading." But it's also the skill that helps us set goals and "see" things both from our past and into our future. It's the picture inside your head—with the sound turned off.

Why

Research in the area of visualization is embedded in the extensive body of literature on memory and memory techniques. To learn, grow, and develop, we must first be able to retain and then recall from memory that which is inherent to our learning. And, just as memory is an essential element in all learning, visualization is an essential element in the memory system. Perhaps the best known book is *The Memory Book*, by Harry Lorayne (1974), in which he explores the device of the mind that we use to recall or remember things. To simplify his comprehensive work, one technique he advocates is referred to as ACE ... ACTION, COLOR, EXAGGERATION. He suggests that as we try to picture or visualize something, we need to create vivid images that have action, color, and exaggerated features in order to better remember it.

In addition to the critical role visualization plays in remembering things from the past, it plays an equally important role in helping us see and plan the future. To recall a mental image of something previously seen is one beginning level of the visualization skill, while imaging an

VISUALIZATION

unknown future event is yet another feature of this ability to picture things mentally. Both are necessary. In the first case, visualization is used to recall and reconstruct, and in the second instance, visualization is used to imagine, invent, and construct new ideas. Specifically, visualization skills are used in reading to construct meaning, in goal setting as we imagine a future time, and in creative endeavors as we invent the unknown. The ability to conjure up an image stimulates long-term learning because that image imprints on the mind and enhances the verbalization process of learning. Images and words together create a more powerful learning episode.

The easiest way to learn to visualize is to practice imagining ideas in your head. Begin by recalling familiar things. Try imagining the following:

Does your bedroom door open into the bedroom or out into the hall?

Which way does Lincoln face on the penny?

Are the stripes on the zebra horizontal or vertical?

What's on the top shelf of your refrigerator?

Remember those images that you have seen many times. Just try to reconstruct a picture in your mind's eye.

Now, after trying these recall exercises, try a more difficult level of visualization. Imagine a character from a recent novel or story. Image every detail including body type, posture, facial expression, coloring, distinguishing marks, clothing, and style. Or, imagine yourself with a new haircut. Imagine your living room with different wallpaper and drapes.

Again, move to an even more difficult level of visualization. Try to see yourself six months from now; six years from now. Do some goal setting and imagine where you'll be and what you'll be doing in a future time. Try to picture the details by elaborating on the initial image.

VISUALIZATION

Try to hold the picture in your mind. For an even more difficult task, after waking, try to recapture the images from your dreams. Concentrate until a dream is in focus. Notice if your dream is in black and white or in color.

———◆———

en Visualization is a skill that can be effectively used as a planning tool and an anticipation strategy. Students can be instructed in the skill of visualization and then directed to use it at the appropriate time. The more often the skill is used, the more proficient students become in using it. For example, ask students to practice remembering something simple, such as a phone number, by mentally picturing it rather than writing it down. This is a quick and easy practice technique that can be used all the time. Instruct students to try visualizing their spelling or vocabulary words, or to notice when they know a word is spelled incorrectly because, "It just doesn't look right." Help them through these "quickies" to become acutely aware of how often they call on the mind's eye to help them know something.

In a more formal approach to visualization, ask students to draw their ideas or map their perception of things. Give them opportunities to use graphic organizers such as webs, Venn diagrams, and concept maps as thinking tools that tap into the visual/spatial intelligence that Howard Gardner (1983) identifies. The use of graphic representations in science, social studies, language arts, and even in the P.E. class (e.g., football diagrams) present ample opportunities to develop this visualization technique.

One Idea

 Use visualization as a planning strategy in a physical education class, in which students are involved in problem solving and goal setting for a personal health and fitness program. Students are asked to visualize themselves as they want to be at the end of the quarter, semester, or year.

Tell them to draw themselves as they look and feel today. See themselves in their mind's eye and then put their ideas on paper.

Then, after developing a comprehensive plan for health and fitness, ask them to draw their vision of a future self. What will they look like after the "transformation" and how will they feel?

BEFORE	AFTER

My Idea

Jot down one idea for this metacognitive tool.

_____

_____

_____

_____

_____

_____

_____

_____

_____

_____

_____

_____

_____

_____

My Reflection

What I Did

Log your use of the idea. Explain what you actually did, giving some details but mostly just the "big idea."

_____

_____

_____

_____

_____

_____

_____

_____

_____

_____

_____

_____

What I Think

Reflect on the activity. What are the pluses and minuses? What other thoughts do you have?

_____

_____

_____

_____

_____

_____

_____

_____

_____

_____

_____

_____

Afterthoughts

_____

_____

_____

_____

_____

_____

_____

_____

_____

_____

_____

_____

_____

_____

_____

_____

_____

_____

_____

STRATEGY 4

Fat and Skinny Questions

[HIGHER-ORDER QUESTIONS]

HIGHER-ORDER QUESTIONS

The concept of fat and skinny questions is really quite simple. Sometimes, questions are fat, full of implications and innuendoes. Other questions are extremely straightforward, cut and dried, with no extenuating ideas or implied ideas. Fat questions call for elaborated answers, full of examples and details; while skinny questions, by their very nature, demand candid, to-the-point answers that often fall into the yes, no, maybe so categories of short-response questions. To illustrate the difference, note the following examples of questions that can be categorized as fat and skinny questions:

FAT	SKINNY
How does this remind you of something you already know?	What does this remind you of?
Why is this a good idea?	Do you think this is a good idea?
What if you were to use this idea tomorrow?	Can you use this idea?
How might you organize this information?	Can you organize this information differently?

By emphasizing the differences in the type of questions, we cue students to recognize those differences. In doing this, we actually make them aware that there are various types of questions and that they can consciously select the kind of question most appropriate to the situation.

Based on Bloom's *Taxonomy of Educational Objectives* (1956), the concept of higher-order thinking suggests that when one is required to analyze, synthesize, or evaluate information, the mind is more engaged in complex thinking than when one is merely asked to recall facts or comprehend or use an idea. This seminal work in cognitive instruction has laid the groundwork for a multitude of related ideas that range from test making to test taking.

HIGHER-ORDER QUESTIONS

However, the essence of Bloom's work lies in the realm of higher-order cognitive tasks that challenge the learner and expand the mind. More recent work in this area includes the Three-Story Intellect model of Fogarty and Bellanca (1987) of gathering, processing, and applying data. The Three-Story Intellect is based on the metaphor developed by Oliver Wendell Holmes in his 1889 book, *The Poet at the Breakfast Table*:

> There are one-story intellects, two-story intellects, and three-story intellects with skylights. All fact collectors, who have no aim beyond their facts, are one-story men. Two-story men compare, reason, generalize, using the labors of the fact collectors as well as their own. Three-story men idealize, imagine, predict—their best illumination comes from above, through the skylight.

The poem suggests the various levels of student thinking that can be triggered: Level one is the "gathering" stage, in which students pull together facts and data; level two is the "processing" stage, in which they make sense of the data; and level three is the "applying" stage, in which students can use their new learnings in relevant ways.

The fat and skinny questioning strategy enables student thinking at the various levels. Skinny questions prompt level one thinking for data collection, while levels two and three are engaged by fat questions that require complex processing and transfer of learning.

 Perhaps the most obvious way to initiate the idea of fat and skinny questions is for the teacher to not only model the questioning in classroom interactions, but to also label the questions as fat or skinny. To explain the idea further, skinny questions often begin with words like *what, where, who,* and *when,* while fat questions might begin with *why* and *how.* Often, the data of the skinny question are inherent in the fat question.

HIGHER-ORDER QUESTIONS

For example, teachers might ask skinny questions such as: What is the title of the film? Where might I find that information? Who is the novelist? When was that episode? On the other hand, teachers might ask fat questions such as: Why do you think that? Why is that so? How might you explain that? How is this situation similar (or different) to that situation?

Once students are introduced to the idea of fat and skinny questions through modeling and labeling, the teacher can then fashion exercises in which students identify, generate, and evaluate their fat and skinny questions. An initial activity may involve students in simply identifying fat and skinny questions at the end of a chapter in the text. For example, one exercise that is especially motivating for kids is to instruct them to work in pairs and to look over the questions at the end of the chapter, prior to reading the text. Then, after reviewing the questions, they are to identify the fat questions and to try and answer only those questions before they read. Of course, they usually will only find about twenty percent of the questions are fat, while eighty percent are skinny.

One opportunity for students to generate fat questions is in the interview process. One idea is to arrange for the students to interview someone at a retirement community or nursing home, write a biography of that person's life, and then present the "adopted grandparent" in a complete book telling the story of his or her life. In order to do this, the students' interview questions must be "fat and fertile."

To designate one time that is more appropriate than another in the strategy of fat and skinny questions is difficult, since questioning interactions are such a major part of the school day. However, it is fair to say that the more often the fat question is used, the better; the more divergent and open-ended the question is, the more likely that students will reason and think through an idea; also the more likely students will respond with depth and originality. In addition, fat and skinny questions are great starters for planning and prelearning activities.

One Idea

Practice generating and discriminating between fat and skinny questions with your class by asking a student volunteer to be interviewed. Use a T-chart on the overhead or chalkboard to record the questions under the proper heading— fat or skinny.

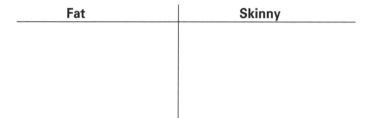

Fat	Skinny

After the question is asked, have the class determine whether it is a fat or skinny question. Record the question in the proper column, and have the child being interviewed answer the question. Call on several students to ask questions. Midway through the interview, ask students to tell you if they notice a difference in the interviewee's answers. How does he or she answer a fat question? How does he or she answer a skinny question? When do you learn the most about him or her, with a fat or skinny question? Ask students if they had to write an interview, which questions would give them the most information— fat or skinny?

If your students need more practice, they may work in groups to interview each other, or you may invite the principal to the classroom for questioning. For additional metacognitive reflection, ask students to answer these questions:
1. Which type of question do you prefer? Why?
2. Do you prefer to ask fat or skinny questions?
3. Do you prefer to answer fat or skinny questions?

From Bellanca & Fogarty (1991), p. 41

My Idea

Jot down one idea for this metacognitive tool.

_____

_____

_____

_____

_____

_____

_____

_____

_____

_____

_____

_____

_____

_____

My Reflection

What I Did

Log your use of the idea. Explain what you actually did, giving some details but mostly just the "big idea."

_____

_____

_____

_____

_____

_____

_____

_____

_____

_____

_____

_____

_____

_____

What I Think

Reflect on the activity. What are the pluses and minuses? What other thoughts do you have?

_____

_____

_____

_____

_____

_____

_____

_____

_____

_____

_____

_____

_____

_____

Afterthoughts

_____

_____

_____

_____

_____

_____

_____

_____

_____

_____

_____

_____

_____

_____

_____

_____

_____

_____

_____

STRATEGY 5

Roll the Dice

[PREDICTING]

PREDICTING

at Predicting is a discrete microskill of thinking—a creative skill that requires the learners to go beyond the given information to make forecasts. Predictions are made all the time. Among the synonyms for predicting are: anticipating, hypothesizing, guessing, inferring, extrapolating, and forecasting. Predictions permeate our lives. For example, we predict the weather on a daily basis; we predict whether or not we can make it through the yellow light; we predict in goal setting where we will be next year in our career or in school. Predictions are a part of everything we do, including simple predictions about the film we're about to see or the book we just started.

Throughout the course of a day, the mind is constantly gathering information, processing that information, and using it to make reasonable predictions. Typical situations that stimulate the prediction process are: predicting someone's reaction to an idea; predicting the outcome of some event; and predicting what might happen next. And in each of these examples, the mental process is quite similar. Based on the facts or information we have, we think of what will probably happen or what might possibly happen. Then, using our common sense, we predict or bet on the idea most likely to occur. Students can learn the BET strategy to make predictions.

B   Base on facts or information at hand.

E   Express probabilities and possibilities.

T   Tender your bet by taking a guess.

———————◆———————

hy Grounded in the research base of reading literature, the concept of activating prior knowledge is addressed by the authors of *Becoming a Nation of Readers* (1984). The premise is that reading is a constructive process and that each reader must connect new information to existing data. This personal context of each learner is referred to as a "schemata." Everyone has a personal cognitive map or schemata that must be reshaped to internalize new information.

PREDICTING

Just as reading is a strategic and constructive process, so too is all learning. By activating prior knowledge, students are mentally prepared to connect incoming information to their past experiences. Ausubel (1981) promotes this idea of advance organizers in a seminal book on cognitive instruction called *Reading in the Content Areas.* For example, he addresses the idea of using a structured overview prior to reading a science chapter. Another researcher, well known in this area, is Anne Brown, who suggests that the constructive process of learning can be accessed through the strategic nature of metacognitive questioning and discussion. The frequent use of the prediction strategy helps students mentally prepare for learning. In turn, it helps learners begin the process of construction by providing needed scaffolding before the structure can be completed.

***

How

How might teachers use predictions in planning and goal setting with students as a metacognitive reflection tool? Without knowing it, of course, students already use prediction. However, the purpose here is to begin incorporating the prediction strategy in more deliberate and intentional ways—ways that help to enhance student awareness of the power of practicing and making predictions.

An example of prediction in a typical classroom setting might be asking students to predict what the results will be on an upcoming test; or letting them predict the outcome in an experiment. Prediction skills are embedded in goal setting, also. For example, in a P.E. class at a local high school, students are given a fitness evaluation: strength, endurance, fat content, cardiovascular fitness, and flexibility. Following the initial evaluation and based on the information and data gathered, students, with the help of the teacher, set goals and develop an exercise plan for the next quarter. In doing so, they must make predictions about how the exercise plan will impact their overall fitness. At the end of the quarter, they are rescreened and their grade reflects how well they met their goals. While this is an unusual illustration, it does show the relationship between predicting and goal setting.

In a more commonly used situation, prediction is used to anticipate what will happen next in a text reading and what is a reasonable answer in a math problem.

PREDICTING

Prediction as a planning strategy is useful in both formal and informal situations. Students can use prediction in basic situations such as predicting difficulties with their homework assignments. Or students can predict what they think an upcoming assembly program will be about. Young children in the primary cluster can make predictions about their trip to the zoo: the funniest animal, the smelliest, the biggest, or the scariest. The opportunities for predicting present themselves throughout the day. Once you focus on the strategy, it will become a natural focus activity that is easily incorporated into a number of learning situations.

Another effective use of prediction in the multimedia classroom is in the use of films, videos, or tape recordings. Run a bit of film or tape with the sound and/or music. Then turn it off and ask students to make predictions on the film or tape based on what they have just seen and heard in the preview. This is an especially impressive use of prediction, because students are using a number of senses to evaluate the input.

Predictions, of course, are easily incorporated in all curriculum areas: science experiments, current events in social studies, reasonable answers in math, and possible scenarios in literature. Prediction is truly a skill of life.

One Idea

 Here is an exercise in prediction students will love to complete—it involves watching their favorite TV show. If possible, younger students can have a parent monitor them completing this assignment. Students tell the teacher which show they wish to watch in order to make a prediction as to how it will end. For the activity, students can complete a sort of lab report during the course of the show. They watch the first segment of the show and at the first commercial, write down a prediction for what will happen next. They must write down a reason why they made the prediction they did. They continue altering and making predictions at each commercial break as the show progresses. At the end of the show, they can determine if their predictions were on track or not. Students can discuss their predictions in class the following day. Those who watched the same program might find it interesting to see if any of their predictions were the same.

YOU CAN BET ON IT . . . TV Predictions	
Commercial Break	What will happen next? When?
#1	
#2	
#3	
#4	
#5	

My Idea

Jot down one idea for this metacognitive tool.

_____

_____

_____

_____

_____

_____

_____

_____

_____

_____

_____

_____

_____

_____

My Reflection

What I Did

Log your use of the idea. Explain what you actually did, giving some details but mostly just the "big idea."

_____

_____

_____

_____

_____

_____

_____

_____

_____

_____

_____

_____

_____

What I Think

Reflect on the activity. What are the pluses and minuses? What other thoughts do you have?

_____

_____

_____

_____

_____

_____

_____

_____

_____

_____

_____

_____

_____

Afterthoughts

STRATEGY 6

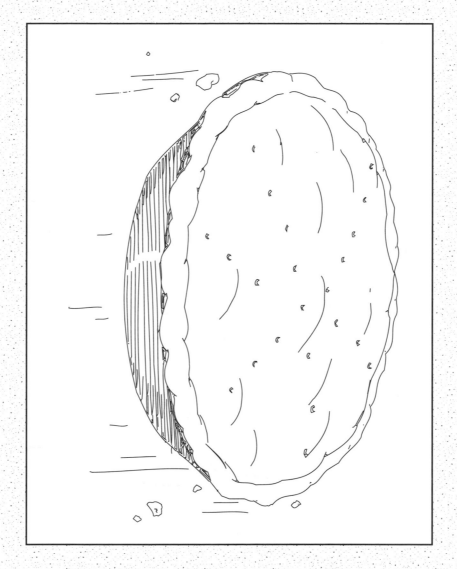

Pie in the Face

[MAKING INFERENCES]

MAKING INFERENCES

 Inferring . . . going beyond the given information, second guessing; implying or reading between the lines. Used as a metacognitive tool, inferring is a way to get students to think about their thinking and to think about what is observed and what conclusions can be drawn from those observations.

It is a difficult and sophisticated skill to differentiate between what is actually observed and what is sometimes inferred. Often the lines become quite blurred. Scientists sometimes have to retract a report because other experts feel that the observational data is laced with inappropriate inferences.

To teach students to become more aware of inferring as a metacognitive strategy, use the example of a typical comic strip. Leave the first and last frames blank. In the center frame, show a woman, aghast, as she opens a wrapped package. Then, ask the students to infer what might have happened in the first frame.

They may say such things as:

She found the package on her front step.

She had a fight with her husband.

She was given the package by her class.

She picked up the wrong package at the counter.

Another example of inferring is to have students read body language or facial expressions and make inferences about them, for example, crossed arms and hands on hips.

In any case, the idea of inferring needs more than just an explanation. It needs an illustration. Once students are clear about exactly what an inference is, then you can begin to look for opportunities to use inferring in your lessons.

MAKING INFERENCES

hy According to the literature in the reading area, the ability to infer is closely connected to the ability to read and comprehend. Based on the seminal work, *Becoming a Nation of Readers* (1984), the authors point out the distinct advantages of reading the primary piece, the original literature or prose as written by the author, versus reading the sterile language of the basal readers. They suggest that the authentic words of the author allow far greater opportunity to understand what the author is implying than the basic, colorless vocabulary of the leveled material. For instance they cite their example:

(original)
One morning Little Hippo felt cross. 'I don't want
lily pads and corn,' he grumbled. 'I wish the hippos
wouldn't watch everything I do.'
(rewritten)
One morning Little Hippo said to himself, 'I don't
want anyone to bring me food.' 'I don't want anyone
to take care of me.'
(Anderson et al., 1984, p. 64-65)

Aligned with the constructivist's view of learning, which sees the learner actively constructing meaning, making sense of the world by connecting new learning to what is already known, this skill of inferring is one of the critical cognitive pieces in the puzzle. Learners must, according to constructivists, construct knowledge for themselves based on their own personal schemata, and "reading between the lines" is part of that process.

In addition to this research, there is some literature in the field of social psychology that suggests that those people who cannot infer well have difficulty in social settings because they are unable to "read" other people. They do not see beyond the literal; they tend to see things at face value, without looking beyond the surface. Other people are seen as having a neutral effect. Therefore, people who cannot infer well may be taken in because they miss the hidden agenda or the ulterior motives of others.

Again, the rationale for teaching students the metacognitive strategy of making inferences is to help them see and understand the subtleties of their interactions in the world around them. This heightened awareness of looking beyond initial impressions enhances their understanding of the world.

MAKING INFERENCES

How

To introduce the inferring strategy, I use a lesson from an old science text (the name of which I have long forgotten). In this text, the students are progressively shown a series of three picture frames and asked to write their observations and then write their inferences.

The frames look something like this:

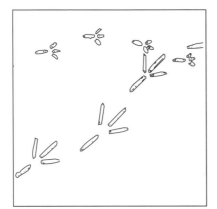 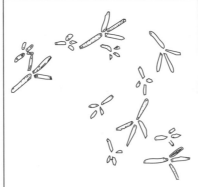 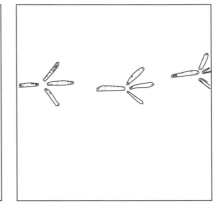

Each of the frames is revealed in sequence, beginning with frame one and moving to frame three. After each frame, students are asked to list some of their observations. Then, based on the observations, they are to make some inferences about the story the tracks tell. For example, they may make the observation that there are two sets of tracks, one large and one small. Then, they might infer about the species of birds. Inferring from the observed data and what they already know about the woods in winter, etc., the students go on to construct understanding or meaning about the frames.

Interestingly, they often infer from the tracks that the large bird *ate* the smaller bird, but just as often, someone will infer that the smaller bird flew away or that the big bird is carrying the smaller one on its back. It is certainly a teachable moment in which discussion flourishes about the fate of the two birds.

With this highly motivating activity, students have an opportunity to look at the distinction between observation and inference; a distinction that is sometimes difficult to discern. However, from the constructivist's view, merely stating observations is a low-level intellectual task, while inferencing requires the learner to search for meaning and to make sense of the observation. This metacognitive task requires the learner to reflect on the given information

MAKING INFERENCES

and tie in to other existing data in the mind; to fold the observed data in with the already known information. Much like folding the chocolate syrup into the cake batter to create a marbled effect, the new images are folded into existing ones to create a new piece; in essence, knowledge has been created or constructed by the learner.

Using this as an introduction to inferring as a metacognitive tool in which the learner continually goes beyond the given information or initial stimulus to make meaning of the data, constructing new knowledge for themselves, you are now able to ask students to infer about lots of things. For example, they can infer your mood from your body language, facial expression, or the tone of your voice. They can infer about the setting of a story from the images in their minds. Or they can infer about the causes of a situation based on the known circumstances.

The important thing is to help students see the value in reflecting on observed data in order to gain a better understanding of what is really going on. This metacognitive behavior is essential if they are to become skilled observers, thinkers, problem solvers, and decision makers. Remember, the opportunities are many, both in formal and informal settings throughout the school day for students to practice constructing meaning by making inferences.

Particularly, as a planning strategy, the use of inferring helps students to set the stage prior to a learning situation. With an increased awareness about making inferences, students show an amazing aptitude for using this tool to interpret their world.

———————◆———————

hen As with many of the reflective tools discussed in this section, inferring often precedes the formal learning situation. And the use of inferring need not be intense or overly complicated. In fact, frequent opportunities to use inferring in and out of the classroom are preferred to a few extensive uses. That is to say, the more often students are led into situations in which they are explicitly asked to infer meaning, the more likely they are to adopt it as a personal strategy in situations that are no longer teacher guided.

One Idea

 An enjoyable and educational way to practice drawing inferences with your students is to use works of art. Students will not only improve their skills in drawing inferences, but will be exposed to masterpieces from the art world. Ask your librarian or media specialist for help in obtaining some pictures of thought-provoking paintings. *Masterpieces of American Painting* by Leonard Everett Fisher contains a few examples that will work, as does any art book.

Explain that before they come to any conclusions, the first step is to make observations. Show them *The Gulf Stream* by Winslow Homer and ask them to make several observations about the painting. They might say:

> The man is surrounded by sharks.
> The ocean looks very rough and the sky looks stormy.
> There is a bigger boat off in the distance.
> The sharks look hungry.
> The sail broke off the boat.

After the class is satisfied with a list of observations, have them take a minute to read through their notes. Then, explain that based on their observations from the picture, they are to make some inferences about the observations. Students may also draw a before and/or after picture of their own, illustrating their inferences.

You can repeat this activity with several paintings for added practice.

My Idea

Jot down one idea for this metacognitive tool.

_____

_____

_____

_____

_____

_____

_____

_____

_____

_____

_____

_____

_____

_____

My Reflection

What I Did

Log your use of the idea. Explain what you actually did, giving some details but mostly just the "big idea."

_____

_____

_____

_____

_____

_____

_____

_____

_____

_____

_____

_____

_____

_____

What I Think

Reflect on the activity. What are the pluses and minuses? What other thoughts do you have?

_____

_____

_____

_____

_____

_____

_____

_____

_____

_____

_____

_____

_____

_____

Afterthoughts

_____

_____

_____

_____

_____

_____

_____

_____

_____

_____

_____

_____

_____

_____

_____

_____

_____

_____

_____

_____

STRATEGY 7

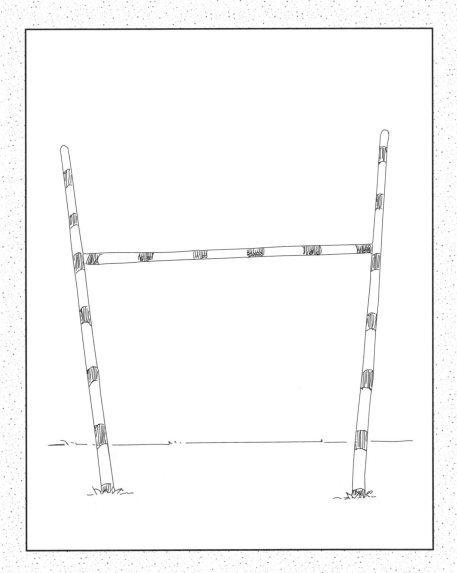

The Goal Post

[GOAL SETTING]

GOAL SETTING

What Goal setting is simply the act of planning desired benchmarks in one's personal or professional life. These goals may be short-term objectives such as finishing a good book or cleaning out a long-forgotten garage or attic. Likewise, the goals may be long term, such as completing a college degree or purchasing a home. In fact, goals may be lifelong yearnings, such as serving others or leaving a legacy to your children. Whatever the form, goal setting is a self-determining process in which one deliberately focuses on the future and makes explicit decisions to accomplish something specific; to work toward established goals or objectives. Setting goals is much like planning a trip. Preparation for the trip precedes actualization of the goal—which is, in this case, to reach a predetermined destination. Also, there may be a number of milestones or mile markers along the way in order to reach the ultimate destination. For instance, intermediate goals may be to travel 400 miles a day or to drive for eight hours each day.

Why The power of setting goals in writing is discussed in almost every self-help book on the market. The literature is chock full of examples of this metacognitive tool of setting goals that are achievable, believable, and conceivable. From Garfield's principles of success in his best-selling book, *Peak Performers* (1986), for the elite athlete to Blanchard's advice for business leaders in *The One Minute Manager* (1982), the concept of goal setting as a success-oriented strategy remains basically unchallenged.

For those who have implemented goal setting as a way of life, their stories chronicle that once something is conceived in the mind, many things come together and cause that goal to be realized. Sometimes, the actual achievement takes longer than initially planned, but without fail, written goals somehow, eventually become accomplished goals or benchmarks in life. There seems to be something about the writing of the goals that creates an indelible mark on the mind. Sometimes, even when we are not consciously monitoring our progress, things

GOAL SETTING

continue to direct us toward the goal. It seems that our actions, which may have appeared incidental, were really quite purposeful in moving us along.

———◆———

How
To help students incorporate the strategy of goal setting into their school day and eventually into their whole day, you simply guide the action of actually thinking about and writing down their goals. Begin with short-term goals such as homework or daily priorities, and then move to more difficult goal-setting sessions in which students look ahead and try to envision achieving a goal that takes more time and effort. A basic example of this might be a fitness goal that involves weight loss over a period of a few months or preparing for and running in a 10K marathon. At some point, you engage students in truly long-range goal setting, such as applying to and getting accepted to a college of their choice or planning for a future career shift by exploring and investigating interests and needs that will be necessary in order to make the desired move.

Often this focus on goal setting begins verbally by asking students to make a *"to-do"* list. To follow up on this informal goal-setting technique, have them question each other the next day about the success of their plans. Just in the telling, students seem to increase their chances of actually doing what they said they would do. Then, once they are familiar with the idea of setting a goal and evaluating their progress in meeting that goal, you introduce the more formal strategy of writing their goals down on paper in a journal or notebook.

Goal setting begins with small, manageable chunks; one day at a time as they say; or one step at a time. Then, these small achievements set in place a string of successes that are easy to replicate. For example, helping students think about and write down their goals for getting their homework done for just that night is a manageable chunk; or agreeing on a set time to have finished reading a book or completing a paper are typical academic goals. These goals are short term and when completed, they readily provide the positive feedback that reinforces these behaviors.

GOAL SETTING

In addition to short-term, more easily attainable goals, students can learn to make more long-term goals that require intermittent monitoring. An example of a long-term goal might be the student who begins swimming lessons, with the goal in mind of joining the swim team when he becomes eligible in sixth grade. Another example of a long-term goal is the student who decides to take drum lessons so she can join the school band. These are goals that do not happen overnight. These are goals that require consistent and persistent attention. Long-term goals often require effort in small bits, spaced over time. Attainment of the goal is gradual and progress builds slowly. These increments may be measurable toward the end goal or they may be implied stepping stones that follow a path toward the end goal.

However, whether the goals are long term or short term, the key to achieving them seems to lie in the planning process. When we first set our mind to something, take the time to articulate it in writing, and put it out there as an explicit target of our actions, somehow, the mind gathers the various factors together to bring the goal into reality. It is this explicit planning process that must be taught to students for them to become metacognitive about using goal setting as a positive tool in their lives.

———◆———

Start small, with daily or even hourly goals. Have students monitor their own progress and track their goal-setting successes. Then, eventually, lead them to goals that are more long range in nature. Finally, have students set goals for both in-school and out-of-school projects, so that formal goal setting becomes part of their repertoire of metacognitive thinking strategies. Use goal setting as a planning strategy whenever the opportunity arises in the classroom, but be sure to include some discussion about why goal setting is an important component in their planning processes. It is through these discussions that students become aware that they can add goal setting to their repertoire of thinking strategies.

A plan to start might be at the introduction of a new unit of study or at the beginning of each week or month. Beginnings of things, in general, seem to be the most appropriate time to use goal setting. Just as we use the new year as a time to make resolutions, the beginning of the unit, week, month, or semester beckons us to make fresh starts with written goals.

One Idea

After discussing the importance of goal setting and how it can help to realize significant achievements, ask students to set some goals of their own. Ask them to set and record one academic target for the week. This can include completing all homework or passing a test or quiz. Next, have students record a higher academic goal for the month. Also, ask them to record a personal ambition for the week and one for the entire month. Allow students ample time to reflect on their goals, jotting down notes and feelings concerning ways to achieve them. Tell them to consider these questions: How will I go about achieving these goals? What benefits will I enjoy by achieving these goals? How will I feel if I succeed? How will I feel if I fail?

Encourage students to share their aims with a partner. By discussing these goals, perhaps other students can give them additional ideas for how to achieve them. Have students throughout the upcoming week and month, check with their partners to see how they are progressing toward their goals while providing encouragement and support to each other.

Upon completion of the first week, hold a class discussion to determine how well people are progressing and what can be done to help others reach their goals. Ask students to reflect for a moment and then discuss what is working and what is not with the class. Repeat this discussion at the end of the month.

My Idea

Jot down one idea for this metacognitive tool.

_____

_____

_____

_____

_____

_____

_____

_____

_____

_____

_____

_____

_____

_____

_____

My Reflection

What I Did

Log your use of the idea. Explain what you actually did, giving some details but mostly just the "big idea."

_____

_____

_____

_____

_____

_____

_____

_____

_____

_____

_____

_____

_____

_____

What I Think

Reflect on the activity. What are the pluses and minuses? What other thoughts do you have?

_____

_____

_____

_____

_____

_____

_____

_____

_____

_____

_____

_____

_____

_____

Afterthoughts

_____

_____

_____

_____

_____

_____

_____

_____

_____

_____

_____

_____

_____

_____

_____

_____

STRATEGY 8

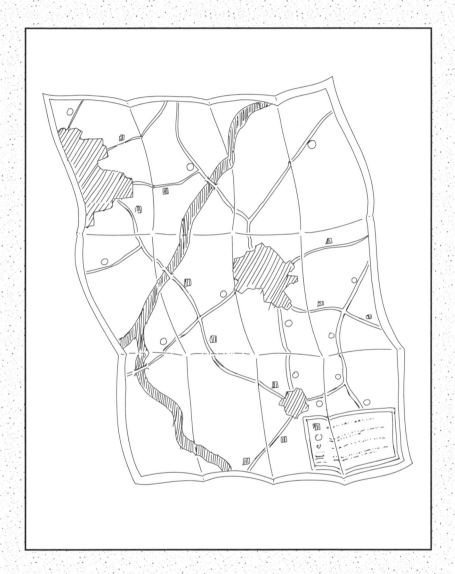

A Road Map

[STRATEGIC PLANNING]

STRATEGIC PLANNING

The concept of a strategic plan implies "over time." In this concept, the operative word is strategic. Strategic implies that the plan is not only intentional but incrementally mapped out with very specific benchmarks that indicate the progress of the plan. Also implied in the concept of strategic planning is the need for assessment, revision, and realignment as progress is measured against the established benchmarks. For example, in constructing a strategic plan for a research project, the work is divided into several manageable chunks that are then assigned an appropriate spot on an envisioned timeline. These designated goals become the incremental benchmarks that indicate the status of the strategic plan.

RESEARCH PROJECT: BENCHMARKS

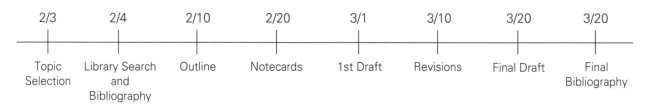

In this illustration, the benchmarks are merely due dates, but criteria can easily be assigned to each due date. For example, the topic selection can indicate a brainstormed list of twenty ideas, labeled "too narrow," "too broad" or "reasonable focus"; the library search can indicate five books, fifteen articles, and two interviews.

Topic Selection	Too Narrow	Too Broad	Reasonable Focus

The distinguishing factors between a plan and a strategic plan are the benchmarks that allow for measurable increments. The benchmarks create intermediate spots along the path that help gauge progress. Benchmarks provide those manageable chunks that help us know where we are in relation to where we indicated we wanted to be.

STRATEGIC PLANNING

 Tom Peters and Nancy Austin talk about strategic planning in their landmark book, *Thriving on Chaos* (1987), as a dynamic, fluid tool that flexes with the constantly changing organization. They applaud the use of deliberate, strategic planning, but emphasize the need to tailor the plan as it unfolds within the dynamic environment of the organization. Thriving on chaos itself refers to the lack of constancy in human organization and the need to monitor and check progress continually against the big picture or the strategic plan that guides the day-to-day actions.

Often, books on leadership and management address the concept of strategic planning. In particular, Peter Senge's seminal piece on systemic change *The Fifth Discipline* (1990), sets the stage for deliberate, thoughtful, and strategic planning in schools. His theory suggests that one area of school restructuring causes irrevocable ripples in all other areas. Without strategic planning, systemic change is possible only in the most erratic ways. The strategic plan provides the links to changing the whole system.

 To relate this to more personal strategic planning, Bruce Williams in *More Than 50 Ways to Build Team Consensus* (1993), uses a matrix model to plot a strategic plan. This charting process requires the user to plan things as manageable chunks.

SUMMER VACATION PLAN					
	Section 1 City 1	Section 2 City 2	Section 3 City 3	Section 4 City 4	Section 5 City 5
Idea 1 *Budget*				$150	
Idea 2 *Route*		mountain roads			
Idea 3 *Sites*					museum
Idea 4 *Transport*	plane		train		

STRATEGIC PLANNING

The chart does just that, charts the plan, or strategizes proposed efforts in an intentional and systematic way. The categories vary depending on the content focus of the planning. For example, they may be quarterly goals that represent an annual plan, chapters for a book, or incremental goals for achieving a fitness level. Whatever the plan, strategic planning through the use of charting visually lays out the plan for easy monitoring and periodic shifts in the direction, intention, and attention. It provides the "chunking" that is easy to track and/or shift if necessary. It also forces the user to account for all of the various phases because an empty square or blank is readily noticed on the chart.

 Strategic planning is most appropriate for long-term projects and ideas. But, as with any effective learning tool, the concept is introduced with simple projects such as a summer reading list or a book report. Also, by using strategic planning with home projects, such as a garden, it becomes a motivating entree for student involvement and learning. This also gives students time to concentrate on the strategy rather than the subject matter content, because the focus of the project is familiar to them; it is part of their daily lives.

Another idea is to incorporate strategic planning into the classroom as a group strategy for the entire class before students use it on their own. An example of total group planning might be an outdoor education experience in which students plan activities and goals for the week on a smaller scale or plan a celebration as a culminating activity for a unit of study. Students can become quite metacognitive about planning their projects if teachers guide them into more mindful behaviors.

The teachable moments for strategic planning are many in the typical classroom. However, teachers must structure the activities so the students, rather than the teacher, take responsibility for the plan. For often, it is the teacher who sets the benchmarks, depriving the students of that metacognitive moment. Guide them, yes, but let the students facilitate the plans themselves. Teach them to fish, rather than giving them a fish to eat.

One Idea

Once students grasp the idea of strategic planning, give them the opportunity to experience the process firsthand by planning a class field trip. Remind them not to forget the importance of mapping out their plan and using benchmarks or due dates for the necessary steps. Start the students out with a brainstorming session listing all of the places that they wish to visit. Ask them to decide on the best three and explain how each is related to a subject they are studying. The students can vote on the best trip, choosing one of the three.

Next, prompt students to brainstorm a list of all of the details they need to plan, such as permission slips, transportation, chaperones, lunch facilities, the time and days that the destination is open, and cost. Prompt students to set a timeline for the entire plan starting with the basic gathering of information to the actual date of the field trip. Explain that having the benchmarks built in the timeline will help them stay organized and reach their goal. Also encourage students to use committees in order to share the workload and function more efficiently.

This project may take several weeks and you will want to use class time to allow students to not only gather information but check the progress of their plan. You will also have the opportunity to discuss the strategic planning process along the way. After students have completed their plan and the field trip is complete, evaluate how the trip went and how having a strategic plan helped. Discuss the positives, negatives, and what they would do differently next time. What advice would they give to another class planning a field trip? Ask students to give you examples where they could use this planning process in their own lives.

My Idea

Jot down one idea for this metacognitive tool.

_____

_____

_____

_____

_____

_____

_____

_____

_____

_____

_____

_____

_____

_____

_____

My Reflection

What I Did

Log your use of the idea. Explain what you actually did, giving some details but mostly just the "big idea."

_____

_____

_____

_____

_____

_____

_____

_____

_____

_____

_____

_____

What I Think

Reflect on the activity. What are the pluses and minuses? What other thoughts do you have?

_____

_____

_____

_____

_____

_____

_____

_____

_____

_____

_____

_____

Afterthoughts

_____

_____

_____

_____

_____

_____

_____

_____

_____

_____

_____

_____

_____

_____

_____

_____

STRATEGY 9

Seesaw Thinking

["WHAT-IF" PROBLEM SOLVING]

"WHAT-IF" PROBLEM SOLVING

What We often think of problem solving as a monitoring tool to watch the progress of a project and solve problems as they occur. Problem solving is a valuable planning tool, too. It is useful for anticipating problems that might occur. In predicting possible barriers or glitches that are likely to happen, we can better prepare for the "surprises" that come along. Planning with the posture of a problem solver, looking for situations that might impede progress, is definitely the kind of metacognitive reflection to promote in students. "What-if" problem solving provides the needed search tool for predicting possible scenarios:

1. What if I get a second job?
   Yes, but what if you have to work overtime?
2. What if I decide to buy a new car?
   Yes, but what if you cannot trade in your old one?

An example of problem solving as a metacognitive planning strategy might be students anticipating possible road-blocks as they put together their ideas for their science projects. After deciding on an idea for their project, they look over their plans and anticipate problem areas before they occur. For example, they may look at the availability of resources, the time needed to complete the project, and the actual time available; or they may problem solve specific components of the project that look sketchy, such as is their idea too broad or too narrow? Is it original? Timely? Too costly? etc. For each of these considerations, the prudent student will do some immediate mental problem solving before proceeding and, in the process, save time and energy.

Mental problem solving is a metacognitive tool that engages the mind as an integral part of the creative process. For example, as one creates an idea, the mental processes involved are generative and productive in nature. At the same time, the mind is crucially examining each idea, and analysis and evaluation pop in almost automatically. This teeter-totter effect of creating/critiquing, creating/critiquing is inherent in the creative process. Problem solving—mental problem solving—is a part of the natural flow of thought in the generation of ideas. Yet, this process resembles the proverbial seesaw effect that precedes decision making.

"WHAT-IF" PROBLEM SOLVING

There are numerous recognized models of problem solving: Polya's seminal work *How to Solve It* (1957) in the area of mathematics and problem solving; the scientific method that prevails in the science labs; and the creative problem-solving method of Parnes, *Aha! Insights into Creative Behavior* (1977) in the area of creativity. The mental problem solving cited here, however, is a much more informal model.

The mental problem solving that occurs in the planning stages of any project is inherent in thinking through the ideas. However, the process can be taught explicitly to students so they learn to look for the pros and cons of an idea as the idea unfolds. By alternating between the creative generation of ideas ("what if. . . ?") and the critical analysis of those same ideas ("yes, but. . . ."), students can refine, edit, and modify within the process. This mental problem solving is informal and unrehearsed. Yet by solving small problems along the way and by overcoming the seemingly insignificant barriers as they appear, the likelihood for ultimate success increases.

How To use mental problem solving as a planning tool, a visual organizer helps students to anchor the process internally. One such structure looks like this:

MENTAL SEESAW MODEL

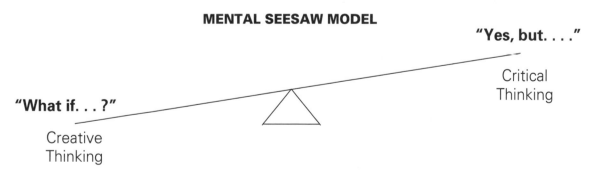

An example might be this advertising idea for local restaurants. *What if I make a video of Chicago restaurants? I'll go in and do a kind of, "Lives of the Rich and Famous," with a panoramic*

"WHAT-IF" PROBLEM SOLVING

view of the place; an interview or statement from the chef and owner; and a testimonial from a satisfied customer.

*   ***Yes, but** who is your audience? And who are your clients; where is the market? How will you keep it current and updated?*

In this model, students experience both perspectives—the positives of the "what if. . . ?" and the negatives or barriers of the "yes, but. . . ." As in de Bono's PMI strategy (Plus, Minus, Interesting), looking at the different angles of a situation provides the basics for good planning and strategic actions. In our minds, we can encounter both sides of an issue and mentally sift out the pros and cons before we plunge into the situation. This "seesaw" approach forces a good look at both sides of an issue. In fact, scanning through the "what if?"/"yes, but" scenarios occurs almost automatically anyway. With this model, the process becomes more deliberate.

 Mental problem solving, using the "what if?/yes, but" seesaw model, is useful as an instructional tool in any problem-based learning situation. By turning the learning episode into a problem to solve, students can easily shift into the mental model.

For example, as teachers develop thematic teaching units, students can shift topical and conceptual themes into questions that pose a universal problem.

Theme	Question
Creativity	a. What if we use: "Why does man create?" b. Yes, but where will it lead the investigation?
Environment	a. What if we look at the upside and downside? Earth: Feast or Famine? b. Yes, but will there be resources for both issues?

These themes, transformed into questions, provide a problem-based learning experience in which students use their mental pictures to plan and sort out their ideas, to experience the seesaw with "what if?"/"yes, but" thinking.

One Idea

 Ask students to use the seesaw model to practice problem-solving skills. As a class, brainstorm a list of items that students view as a problem with their school. Select one issue or problem to deal with and complete the seesaw exercise as a class. For example, high school students might feel that one school problem is inadequate parking. Students can use a seesaw similar to the one provided to examine both sides of the parking issue.

WHAT IF. . . ?   **YES, BUT. . . .**

What if we tried to solve the over-crowded parking situation by issuing permits?

Yes, but who would get the permits and who would award the permits to students?

What if only seniors could use the parking lot?

Yes, but is that fair to underclassmen who have a legitimate reason for driving a car to school?

What if we created more spaces in the parking lot?

Yes, but how would the parking spaces be built and paid for?

Whatever the problem may be, a seesaw chart can help students see both sides of an issue. By weighing the answers against each other they can search more in depth for a solution to a problem rather than rushing into a situation without any forethought.

Once students are comfortable with this process, ask them to use a learning log to record a personal problem of their own in which they used the seesaw chart to find possible solutions.

My Idea

Jot down one idea for this metacognitive tool.

_____

_____

_____

_____

_____

_____

_____

_____

_____

_____

_____

_____

_____

My Reflection

What I Did

Log your use of the idea. Explain what you actually did, giving some details but mostly just the "big idea."

_____

_____

_____

_____

_____

_____

_____

_____

_____

_____

_____

_____

_____

What I Think

Reflect on the activity. What are the pluses and minuses? What other thoughts do you have?

_____

_____

_____

_____

_____

_____

_____

_____

_____

_____

_____

_____

_____

Afterthoughts

_____

_____

_____

_____

_____

_____

_____

_____

_____

_____

_____

_____

_____

_____

_____

_____

STRATEGY 10

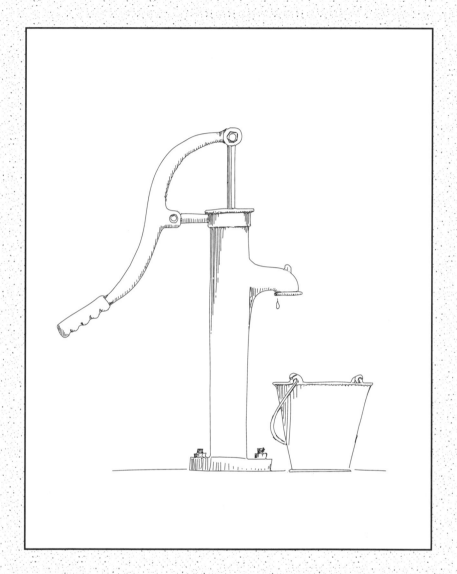

Prime the Pump

[KWL]

K W L

 The KWL is a reading strategy developed by Donna Ogle (1986). **K** stands for What do you **Know?** **W** is for What do you **Want** to know? and **L** is for What have you **Learned?** Obviously, the first two, the "K" and the "W," are strategies for prelearning or for planning prior to the learning unit. The "K" and the "L" set the stage for learning.

The KWL falls into the category of graphic organizers, thinking tools that help make learning visible to the students as they graphically represent their thoughts on paper. Although the KWL was developed in the reading area, graphic organizers are applied in myriad learning situations. As a planning strategy, it is one of the most popular and perhaps, most widely known, next to the web, concept map, and Venn diagram.

Plants

K	W	L
They are alive. They need water. They breathe out O_2 and breathe in CO_2.	Which ones are poisonous? Are mushrooms plants? Which plants did dinosaurs like?	

The research on graphic organizers or advance organizers dates back to Ausubel's structured overviews. Presented in Vacca's book, *Content Area Reading* (1981), graphic representations of the text prior to the reading are suggested to help students predetermine what they are about to read. Although the KWL is attributed to the work of Donna Ogle, there are numerous others including **Venn diagrams, concept maps, flowcharts, matrices, cause and effect circles**, and the **fishbone**. The use of a KWL or similar graphic focuses student attention for more concentrated learning. In fact, without the attention to their own prior knowledge, students have a difficult time making meaning of new information.

Through the process of sorting out what they already know about a topic, students are forced to call up prior knowledge and reorganize their thoughts and connections about it.

KWL

Then, based on facts they already have in the forefront of their minds, students can proceed to focus on other aspects of the topic that they are wondering about or want to know more about.

In summary, the rationale for the KWL is rooted in the constructivist theory of learning that holds that learners make meaning of new facts in relationship to what they already know and want to know. They learn what they are prepared to assimilate into the context of their previous learnings and construct personal meaning that is relevant to them.

How

To implement a KWL in the classroom or staff room, a facilitator prompts thinking about the topic through a typical brainstorming activity. As students recall facts, they are charted under the "K" column of information as things they know already . . . or think they know. As this list is generated, students may challenge a stated fact. (The challenged information can be marked with a question mark.) Remember, this is a prelearning activity that makes student thinking visible. So, even if they state obvious misconceptions, it is important to record them. Later, as the idea is explored more fully, corrections can be made to the chart. But for now, whatever the student thinking is—accurate or inaccurate—at least it is visible.

Once the "Known" facts are gathered, students can begin to pose the questions they have about the topic; the things they are curious about; what they are wondering about or want to explore. These questions are recorded in the "W" column for things they want to know or are wondering about. In fact, these essential questions drive the inquiry and as students listen to each other's ideas, more thoughtful questions evolve.

These two lists set the stage for the learning episodes; prior knowledge is gathered and questions are generated. Now, students enter into the learning activities with defined purposes: they want to see if their facts are right and they want to find specific answers to new questions they've posed. Their interest is piqued for optimal learning.

KWL

The most appropriate use of the KWL strategy in the early grades is probably a full-blown, total group investigation of what they know and what they want to know. Displayed on large butcher paper, the KWL chart is a place to capture as many ideas as possible. By doing this prior to a unit, as an introductory activity, teachers are made aware of the extent of student understanding on the topic. This, of course, helps in tailoring the unit to the needs of each particular group. In addition, it sparks thoughtfulness in students as they approach the new idea and becomes a visible, dynamic chart of that thinking that can be constantly enriched with emerging ideas. Some teachers actually review the chart each day, as they revisit the unit of study. Additional facts are placed under the "K" and emergent questions are placed in the "W" column. In this way, students experience a model of ongoing reflection as they proceed through the unit.

With older students, on the other hand, the KWL may become a journal entry, rather than a large chart. In the journal, students generate their own schemata of what they know and do not know. However, to facilitate student use of the KWL, even with the more mature student, it may be prudent to encourage discussion through partner or small group dialogues or some large group samplings.

K	W	L
What do I **K**now?	What do I **W**ant to know?	What have I **L**earned?

One Idea

 Before starting a unit of study, ask students to complete and share a KWL on the topic. To increase motivation and tap into prior knowledge, ask students to work in small groups and to use the chart to record what they already know and what they want to learn.

Tell students to really think about what they want to know regarding the topic. For example, young students enjoy learning about dinosaurs—usually they bring some amount of prior knowledge to the subject area. However, they are still very curious to learn more. To build intrinsic motivation, tell students that as a class they will all try to study more about dinosaurs to learn the specific answers to their questions. Throughout the unit, remind students to record new facts that they are learning on their KWL chart.

DINOSAURS

K	W	L
Some dinosaurs were meat eaters but most ate plants.	Why did they become extinct?	
Dinosaurs came in all sizes and shapes.	Where did they live?	
Some dinosaurs could fly.	What was the earth like when dinosaurs were alive?	
Dinosaurs lived on land and in the water.	How big were they really?	
Some dinosaur bones have been found.	Were they slimy?	

My Idea

Jot down one idea for this metacognitive tool.

_____

_____

_____

_____

_____

_____

_____

_____

_____

_____

_____

_____

_____

_____

_____

My Reflection

What I Did

Log your use of the idea. Explain what you actually did, giving some details but mostly just the "big idea."

_____

_____

_____

_____

_____

_____

_____

_____

_____

_____

_____

_____

_____

What I Think

Reflect on the activity. What are the pluses and minuses? What other thoughts do you have?

_____

_____

_____

_____

_____

_____

_____

_____

_____

_____

_____

_____

_____

Afterthoughts

_____

_____

_____

_____

_____

_____

_____

_____

_____

_____

_____

_____

_____

_____

_____

SECTION
II

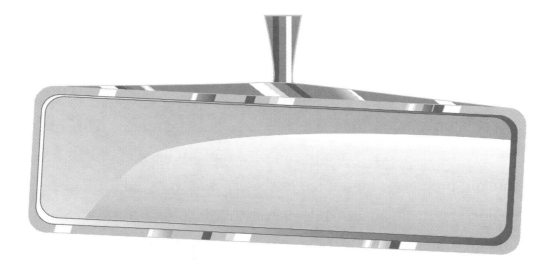

MONITORING

Strategies for Students to Use

Nothing is more terrible than activity without insight.
—Thomas Carlyle

To monitor is to check one's progress; to look over something as it is actually under way; to review a project at various stages while it is still under construction. For example, hall monitors check the activity in the halls while school is in session. There is no need for a monitor when the students are not there because there is nothing to monitor.

By its very nature, monitoring as a reflective, metacognitive activity must differ drastically from the thorough scrutinizing of the planning stage. Just as with the rear-view mirror, progress is monitored as the car is moving; adjustments, whether minor or major, are usually made while the car continues to move. Of course, as the maneuver progresses, one continues to use the reflections provided by the small, adjustable mirror and theoretically progress is benefited by the additional view.

So, too, in the metacognitive reflection of the learners, the continuous, consistent, and deliberate monitoring during the learning allows for constant adjustment and necessary revisions along the way. Perhaps an easy example is that of the person trying to find an unknown address. Although the directions were written down in some sort of a plan, usually either a map or in step-by-step verbal notations, prior to setting out, the driver almost always monitors his or her progress enroute. "Oh, yes! Go past the bank and cross the railroad tracks. . . ." This intermittent monitoring at key check points along the way assures the driver that he or she is on course. And, this momentary reflection, in the midst of the action, often saves lengthy backtracking or irritating stops to call for further instructions.

Monitoring is a skill of metacognition because it requires acute awareness of what is happening, as it is happening. This requires skillful posturing as one stands back from the action and virtually looks in on it—almost as though one were an outsider peering into another's situation. Sometimes, I refer to this as a "freeze frame" to help students separate the action itself, from thinking about the actions. Freeze frame. Stand aside and look over what you are doing; note your progress;

think about how you can improve the situation with minor adjustments or a change of strategies. It is sometimes hard to "change horses midstream," especially when implementation seems so well planned initially, but the change or adjustment is often just what is needed to make the critical difference.

This section includes ten strategies to help students monitor their actions in metacognitive ways—thinking about their behaviors and—even though reluctant to move off course—being able to know when something needs changing and when it is right on track. Among the strategies are: memorizing, mental menus, labeling, thinking aloud, recovery strategies, observation, conferencing, taping, cueing, and transfer strategies.

MONITORING 10

STRATEGIES

1. *Talk to Yourself* [Think Aloud] . . . 93

2. *Soup Cans* [Labeling Behaviors] . . . 103

3. *Alarm Clock* [Recovery Strategies] . . . 111

4. *Instant Replay* [Tape Recordings] . . . 121

5. *Post-it Note* [Memoing] . . . 131

6. *Mental Menus* [Tracking] . . . 139

7. *Cue Cards* [Prompting] . . . 149

8. *Two-Way Talk* [Conferencing] . . . 157

9. *Transfer Talk* [Bridging] . . . 167

10. *The Microscope* [Recorded Observations] . . . 177

STRATEGY 1

Talk to Yourself

[THINK ALOUD]

THINK ALOUD

What The think-aloud strategy is exactly what it says. It is assuming the habit, which is sometimes joked about, of talking aloud to oneself. It is thinking made audible by talking aloud. In fact, the saying, "What goes through his head comes out of his mouth," capsulizes the idea of talking aloud in order to clarify and monitor one's thought processes.

Often, this is illustrated in real-life situations. For example, while following directions to an unknown destination, you might monitor your progress by saying, "I just passed the third light; there's the garage on the corner; two more streets and I'll turn left on Elm."

Or, as one tries to program a VCR to record a program, he or she may repeat the steps aloud to monitor the procedure: "First, find the selection screen. Next, locate the program code. . . ." These monitoring techniques are ways that help us track our thoughts. Each time we verbally make note of a step in the procedure, we are establishing a checkpoint for our thinking.

This strategy is sometimes used in conjunction with the paired-partner technique of cooperative learning. In this version, the paired-partner, problem-solving strategy establishes one partner as the problem solver and the other one as the monitor or questioner. Throughout the problem-solving scenario, the problem solver talks aloud about the problem, stating every thought that comes to bear on the approach to solving the problem. In turn, the monitor asks key or pivotal questions of the problem solver to help guide the thinking toward a viable solution.

In either case, whether alone or in a partner pairing, the think-aloud technique requires constant verbalization of the thought processes. Think it! Say it! Think it! Say it as you think. Make the thinking known through the articulation. Think aloud and hear yourself thinking.

While this strategy may appear simplistic on the surface, the concept of thinking, saying, and then hearing one's ideas actually provides powerful multimodal ways of knowing and learning. The mind has several modes of input that act to reinforce each other. Thinking aloud is thinking in concert with the speaking and listening components of communication.

THINK ALOUD

Bloom, in *All Children Learning* (1956) first looked at this idea of thinking aloud while exploring the idea of improving standard test scores. Whimbey and Lockhead, in *Intelligence Can Be Taught* (1984), present convincing applications. This array of think-aloud strategies used as metacognitive monitoring tools are worthy of attention in cognitive education. They range from the peer editing of the writing group to the complex series of steps involved in solving mathematical equations. Grounded in the theoretical literature in the reading area, Whimbey and Lockhead illustrate how thinking aloud is a viable strategy to use in content area reading as well as in the writing process and in problem solving in general.

The mind is a curious thing; it imprints information in myriad ways. It just makes sense that if one thinks and conceptualizes an idea mentally, and at the same time, verbally traces that series of thoughts aloud, that the two modes will make a more lasting impression on the brain. So as Art Costa says, "If you find yourself talking—to yourself—don't be alarmed, you are only metacognating!" And, to take it one step further, you may want to deliberately "talk to yourself" or encourage your students to talk to themselves as you learn to use this metacognitive tool to monitor and adjust your own thinking.

To implement the think-aloud strategy in the classroom seems simple at the onset. However, to actually develop this as a consistent metacognitive tool for youngsters proves to be a bit more difficult. With that in mind, look at the following introductory techniques for thinking aloud and then at some methods for refining its use for various content and life situations.

To help students begin to think aloud as they work through an idea, model the behavior for them just as you might with a math problem on the board. For each written notation you

THINK ALOUD

make, you also make a verbal notation by telling *what* you are doing and *why* you are doing it. In other words, you are not only thinking aloud about the specific step or computation, but also about the reasoning behind the move. Science lab demonstrations are perfect for this at the middle or upper grades.

For the younger students, another example of an introductory level "talk-aloud" lesson might be a chess game, checker game, or other board game. The teacher models talking aloud by stating every move and the reason for making the move.

This, of course, is not a new strategy for teachers to use as they demonstrate an idea. What is new, however, is that after observing the demonstration, the students are expected to imitate the thinking-aloud behavior. While it sounds simple enough, many novices find it difficult and almost distracting to continually talk their way through a task. On the other hand, other students find it easy and almost comforting to trace their thoughts orally.

Once the idea of thinking aloud has been introduced and practiced once or twice, more formal and long-term procedures are needed to refine the use of this idea. This is where it seems appropriate to use long-term partners. The idea of long term is stressed intentionally— because the student pairs need time to develop as "cognitive partners." They need repeated interactions to become skilled at asking each other the kinds of questions that spur insightfulness in the thinking strategy.

However, do not be fooled by the apparent sophistication of this technique. Even very young children can become more metacognitive in their approach to learning by thinking aloud as they attempt to solve a puzzle or build a model. In fact, if young learners are introduced to thinking aloud early in the schooling process, they become quite adept at revealing the inner workings of their minds as they learn to unravel the more complex problems they encounter.

Of course, coupled with the partner strategy, students also need time alone to practice thinking aloud. Simple situations present themselves in which a problem can be posed such as, "How do you make a paper airplane?" or "Tell me what you are thinking as you edit your essay. Why are you making those choices or decisions?" At times, just by saying something aloud, the learner is startled by the understanding gained through that simple process. Thus, thinking aloud is best accomplished through a formal modeling of the strategy and then repeated opportunities to use it.

THINK ALOUD

hen It seems most appropriate to use the think-aloud strategy in problem-based learning episodes or more typical problem-solving lessons or assignments. Also, knowing that this strategy is more difficult than it seems, students need to be introduced to the think-aloud idea early in the year or semester and then given ample opportunities to practice both individually and with partners.

However, once the students are familiar with it, the classroom or laboratory offers innumerable opportunities for them to incorporate thinking aloud into their repertoire of metacognitive reflection tools. For example, the following chart suggests fertile activities in various subject areas.

MATH	Problem solving
WRITING	Critiquing and revising
READING	Comprehending
TECHNOLOGY	Computer software solutions

One Idea

 The think-aloud strategy forces students to examine how they solve problems and may help them to correct errors. Model how to solve a math problem while thinking out loud for the class. Take any math problem from the textbook students work from. An example is this simple word problem.

If bubble gum costs 50 cents and licorice costs 35 cents, how much money will you need to buy both?

Model your thinking by saying, "The first thing I will do is reread the word problem to make sure I understand it. I notice that the problem wants to know how much it will cost for both candies. This means I need to add them together. I will be using addition." Put a plus sign on the board and an equal sign, writing them in column fashion, rather than horizontally. Now say, "I need to figure out the two things I want to add together: the price of the bubble gum, 50 cents, and the licorice, 35 cents." Put these numbers on either side of the addition sign. "Now I need to add these together. I will start in the ones column. I have 5 ones." Put a 5 in the ones column. "Next I look at the tens column: 5 tens plus 3 tens is 8 tens or eighty." Put the answer in the tens column. "My answer is 85 cents. I will need 85 cents to buy both the bubble gum and licorice."

Next, ask students to complete a math problem on their own using this strategy. Encourage them to whisper to themselves through each step that they are taking and thinking about. Once everyone has completed the problem, ask for a student to volunteer his or her solution as well as how he or she thought aloud. Ask if anyone else found the answer another way— ask that student to model his or her thinking. Students will be amazed how the same problem can be solved in so many ways. Allow students to work in partners or groups, thinking aloud and solving problems multiple ways.

My Idea

Jot down one idea for this metacognitive tool.

_____

_____

_____

_____

_____

_____

_____

_____

_____

_____

_____

_____

_____

_____

_____

_____

My Reflection

What I Did

Log your use of the idea. Explain what you actually did, giving some details but mostly just the "big idea."

_____

_____

_____

_____

_____

_____

_____

_____

_____

_____

_____

_____

_____

_____

What I Think

Reflect on the activity. What are the pluses and minuses? What other thoughts do you have?

_____

_____

_____

_____

_____

_____

_____

_____

_____

_____

_____

_____

_____

_____

Afterthoughts

STRATEGY 2

Soup Cans

[LABELING BEHAVIORS]

LABELING BEHAVIORS

There's a story of a young girl who was asked to be one of the bridesmaids in her cousin's wedding party. As a prank on the newlyweds, the wedding party members sneaked into the kitchen of the newlyweds and removed every label from every can in their cupboard. For months, the young couple unknowingly opened cans of beans when they had hoped for soup or they opened cans of soup when they really wanted vegetables. Just as the label on a can identifies the contents inside, the label on behavior identifies the thinking inside.

Thus, by helping students to recognize, identify, and label their cognitive behaviors, they become cognizant of the inner workings of their mind. By labeling their actions as they act, the labels provide valuable information that monitors their behavior. Just as the "inside trader" in the *stock market* exchanges privileged data with him- or herself to gain an advantage in investing, so too, the "inside trader" in the *classroom* exchanges privileged data with him- or herself to gain an advantage in learning. The inside information in this case, of course, is the awareness and knowledge of what he or she is doing through the labeling process: predicting, classifying, comparing, judging.

An example from the classroom is the student who continually blurts out an idea in the middle of a suspenseful story. While the outburst is disruptive and unfair to the rest of the class, it is also quite insightful and often correct. By labeling the behavior, the predictive nature of student thinking is emphasized and encouraged: "That's good predicting, Joey. Now, let's all think about possible predictions and tell your partner your ideas."

Although there is a great deal of concern in the literature about the detrimental effects of labeling students and subsequent tracking traditions that accompany the labeled youngsters, the labeling discussed here is that of identifying and naming the complex, multifaceted no-

LABELING BEHAVIORS

tion of the thought processes of the mind. The labeling is on the thinking processes, not on the ability of the student. It's labeling in order to identify and understand thinking processes.

Costa quotes Vygotsky (1986) as saying that, "thinking is embedded in the language of the classroom." If this is true, then it may follow that thinking about thinking is embedded in the awareness that comes with language; with the naming or labeling of the type or mode or degree of thinking involved.

Work in the transfer of learning suggests that teachers are more likely to use thinking skills in their classrooms once they have actually labeled the discrete skills (inferring, concluding, generalizing) that occur (Fogarty et al., 1992). Also, a further finding is that teachers who are able to recognize and put a name to a thinking skill, social skill, graphic organizer, or one of the multiple intelligences, will also seek out new ones that they themselves are not currently using. So, just as the labeling of cognitive behaviors leads to more comprehensive transfer for students, labeling cognitive behaviors leads to more comprehensive transfer for teachers, too.

The most expedient way to teach students how to label their cognitive behaviors is to develop a cognitive vocabulary for the classroom. Then, use those words whenever it is appropriate. The next step is to instruct students to begin labeling their own behaviors. For example, during a discussion on the water cycle, students are asked to label the type of thinking they're using:

Example 1: The student tells about a personal experience and labels his thinking: generalizing.

Example 2: The student states a definition of evaporation and its effects and labels his thinking: drawing conclusions.

Example 3: The student draws a diagram on the board of the rain, plants, and stems in the water cycle and labels his thinking: imaging, visualizing.

Example 4: The student creates a jingle in math and labels his multiple intelligence: musical/rhythmic.

Example 5: The student works in a small group, reaches agreement on the country to study, and labels his social skill: reaching consensus.

LABELING BEHAVIORS

Labeling is simply a metacognitive afterthought or footnote to the learning at hand. It is a reflective statement or naming of the interaction that requires one to step back for a moment and make that key observation of what generalizations can be made in terms of the cognitive labels that are appropriate.

Labeling is most likely to happen during the learning experience, in the heat of the action, so to speak. For it is far more powerful to name the behavior as it is occurring rather than before it happens or after it has happened. By recognizing and identifying the thinking mode as it is taking place, the student understands the connection instantly.

It is similar to telling a young child, "Hot! That is the stove. It cooks the food with the heat from flame. It will burn you," as he or she is actually moving toward the stove. Labeling occurs within the context of the action if it is to be effective for the long term. It is embedded in the moment of occurrence, as it is happening.

Also, in terms of the other appropriate times to use the labeling technique for metacognitive reflection, it seems that vicarious incidents such as reading, viewing a video, or watching others in a role play or classroom episode might also offer golden opportunities to reflect upon and label others' cognitive behaviors.

Just as labels are used frequently with young children as they learn about their physical world, labels are used frequently also with students of all ages as they learn about their cognitive world. In both instances, the labels are a first step in the "knowing" process. Of course, the labeling referred to in this case is to help a student "know thyself."

One Idea

 Give students more practice with the labeling strategy by using a role-playing activity. Before class, write five or six typical classroom scenarios that involve dialogue between students and teachers. For example, have students role-play conducting an experiment, holding a discussion in a cooperative group, partners working on a speech, or other common activities done during the course of the school day.

Your scenarios can be very brief but should include examples of a variety of thinking skills. Include skills such as:

generalizing

predicting

classifying

evaluating

inferring

inventing

problem solving

Ask the class to pay particular attention to the student-actors and the kinds of thinking they are demonstrating. After each role play is performed, ask the rest of the class to identify the thinking skills exhibited. Encourage them to give you another example of the skill as well. Discuss how being conscious of the names of these thinking skills will familiarize students of the actual cognitive processes they are using.

My Idea

Jot down one idea for this metacognitive tool.

_____

_____

_____

_____

_____

_____

_____

_____

_____

_____

_____

_____

_____

_____

_____

_____

My Reflection

What I Did

Log your use of the idea. Explain what you actually did, giving some details but mostly just the "big idea."

_____

_____

_____

_____

_____

_____

_____

_____

_____

_____

_____

_____

What I Think

Reflect on the activity. What are the pluses and minuses? What other thoughts do you have?

_____

_____

_____

_____

_____

_____

_____

_____

_____

_____

_____

_____

Afterthoughts

_____

_____

_____

_____

_____

_____

_____

_____

_____

_____

_____

_____

_____

_____

_____

_____

_____

_____

STRATEGY 3

Alarm Clock

[RECOVERY STRATEGIES]

RECOVERY STRATEGIES

Recovery strategies are actions taken to "recover, recapture, or rethink" an idea once the person realizes that something has gone awry. It is the awareness that things are off course that triggers the recovery action. The awareness of a problem or mistake signals to the learner that an alternative approach is needed to recover the missing or misfitting information.

For example, as the student works through a budget problem, he or she notices a disagreement in the monthly totals versus the grand total. Alerted to the mismatch, a recovery strategy is put into operation as the student shifts gears and retraces his or her steps. In this checking process, a discrepancy is found—only eleven months were entered, not the twelve needed to be accounted for—so that calculation begins again.

Recovery strategies occur in every subject area, not just the tedious computations of math. For example, in writing, recovery strategies occur every time you circle back to change a word. Something triggers your brain that the word is *not* exactly the right one; the phrase is a little off, and your meaning is cloudy. And so the mind begins the strategy of recovering the original thought and slotting in the appropriate word or phrase.

In reading, each time you put down the novel and then pick it up again, you must move into a recovery mode—searching, scanning, or recalling where you left off. What was going on? What is about to happen? That is why, in writing, some successful authors provide this hint: *never stop writing until you know what is coming next.* In theory, that facilitates the recovery of your thoughts and speeds the writing along when you next sit down to write again.

Recovery strategies appear in the theoretical literature on metacognition as ways to improve reading skills. Brown (1980) and others notice that good readers are readily aware of a missed idea or a gap in their understanding while reading. These readers immediately shift to some sort of recovery mode—scanning for their place, recording, or simply reflecting for a moment to capture their last thought.

RECOVERY STRATEGIES

This ability to recover and go on allows metacognitive learners to bridge learning from one moment to the next or from one sitting to another. They have the ability to know when *they know* and more importantly, when *they do not know something*. It is this awareness of the interruption in the logic of their thought processes that takes them beyond the cognitive and into the realm of the metacognitive.

This is an important distinction because it is in the contemplative mode that learners take control of their own learning. Remember, when one thinks about his or her thinking, adjustments are made.

While the level of metacognition varies, according to Swartz and Perkins (1989), from tacit to aware, strategic, and then to reflective, it seems that in order to make shifts, one is at best aware and more likely strategic if slight shift changes are utilized to recover a thought or idea in the heat of the action itself.

Fortunately, there is a great deal of research surrounding this idea of cognitive and metacognitive activity. Howard (1994) looks at the mental connections made as one searches for information in the complex technological network available today. Howard's work suggests that by making the mental mapping of the cognitive connections obvious to the learner, the search can be guided *more* metacognitively. Of course, it follows that quick and ready recovery from a "birdwalk" may result from more mindful attention to the various connections made.

To help students become skillful in using the recovery strategies, they must first become aware of gaps or chasms in their learning. They must develop internal signals that sound the alarm, that signal a link in the logic chain is broken or that there is a missing link. This can be done in a number of ways both in the classroom and in other life situations.

However, students need explicit instruction in the different recovery strategies inherent to the various disciplines. Reading strategies that help one recover a thought include: scanning for a familiar phrase; rereading from the beginning; reflecting a moment to capture the idea mentally; or noting a chart or diagram that accompanies the text.

RECOVERY STRATEGIES

In math, however, while some recovery strategies may overlap with those mentioned for reading, most are matched to the discipline itself. For example, in mathematical reasoning, a step-by-step review may be used to recover the logic of an argument. The known is segregated from the unknown in an attempt to recover the mode of inquiry needed. Principles are repeated to see if the applied rule sheds light on the idea.

Although recovery strategies in science may resemble those already noted, some, however, are special to the scientific investigation. An often-used recovery technique in the lab, for example, is a review of the gathered data for insight into an emerging idea or a fleeting idea. A moment to visualize the idea is another common recovery strategy. That focused concentration or time to think may recover the thought.

First, the students must become *aware* of the fact that they have a gap in their understanding. Then, with that awareness, they are able to *control* their learning by shifting into a recovery mode.

———————◆———————

When While tacit metacognitive recovery behavior is implied each time the learner tries "to pick up where he or she left off," in some activities such as reading a magazine article, writing an essay, or completing an interrupted homework assignment, the more sophisticated and subtle use of recovery strategies often requires more technical assistance. Perhaps, the appropriate time to introduce this metacognitive monitoring strategy of recovering an idea is after students have worked with the more explicit *planning* strategies. Once they are familiar with the concept of metacognition and their inner awareness has been piqued, monitoring strategies can be formally introduced. However, students vary greatly in their levels of metacognitive awareness, so monitoring strategies such as recovery strategies may initially require verbal cueing from a facilitator.

Once introduced to recovery strategies as a monitoring technique, students find that long-term assignments, extended projects, and activities that need time are most appropriate

RECOVERY STRATEGIES

for using recovery techniques. Once aware of the benefits of efficiently using recovery strategies, students will employ them in myriad situations, both in school and outside of school.

To facilitate the use of recovery strategies, again, modeling by the teacher is critical. A simple example might be the reading aloud of a novel. Each day, in a third grade classroom, this teacher reads a chapter from *Charlotte's Web*. But, before she begins the new chapter, she takes a moment to review the action from the previous reading.

To make the recovery strategy obvious to students, however, she actually tells them, "we must *recover* the action from yesterday. One way to do that is to reread the last line or two—or we could just concentrate and try to recall what we heard. But, today, let's try to capture the action by just starting to read and see if we can pick up the action."

One Idea

 Make recovery strategies a part of the lesson. When teaching elementary students reading and vocabulary skills, model how to use pictures or illustrations within the story to help them understand the vocabulary. When students stumble upon an unfamiliar word when reading, they can rely on the pictures for a clue. Have students share with their classmates some of their own personal strategies for understanding what they read.

Another recovery strategy that uses pictures is to include drawings in their notes. For example, in biology, older students can read about osmosis in cells and then actually sketch the process. By translating the reading into their own picture, they conceptualize, visualize, and translate their learning.

For older students working with difficult content such as biology, chemistry, or physics you may want to introduce several recovery strategies. Explain that to increase their comprehension of a difficult passage of text, students can stop and take a moment to reflect on their reading.

Do they truly understand what they have just read?

What did they find confusing?

Can they summarize their reading in five or six sentences?

What is the significance of what they are reading?

Stress that students should stop and try to conceptualize or summarize what they have read in their own words.

My Idea

Jot down one idea for this metacognitive tool.

_____

_____

_____

_____

_____

_____

_____

_____

_____

_____

_____

_____

_____

_____

_____

My Reflection

What I Did

Log your use of the idea. Explain what you actually did, giving some details but mostly just the "big idea."

_____

_____

_____

_____

_____

_____

_____

_____

_____

_____

_____

_____

_____

_____

What I Think

Reflect on the activity. What are the pluses and minuses? What other thoughts do you have?

_____

_____

_____

_____

_____

_____

_____

_____

_____

_____

_____

_____

_____

_____

Afterthoughts

_____

_____

_____

_____

_____

_____

_____

_____

_____

_____

_____

_____

_____

_____

_____

STRATEGY 4

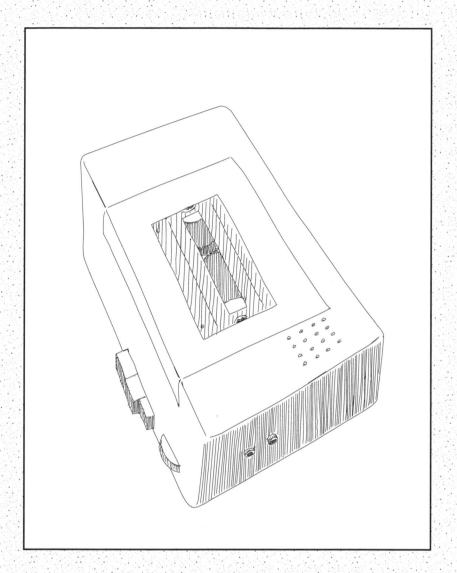

Instant Replay

[TAPE RECORDINGS]

TAPE RECORDINGS

A tape recording of student interactions is a powerful tool in teaching students about metacognition because it is next to impossible for anyone to be cognitive and metacognitive simultaneously. The *novice* needs to learn the technique of metacognition. The *veteran* cannot always afford the luxury of stepping back from the cognitive interaction of the moment and reflecting metacognitively about what took place.

The tape recording of classroom scenarios resembles the popular television technique used in sporting events called "instant replay." For example, immediately following a football play, the studio technicians not only "replay" the segment of tape showing the featured play, but announce again what is happening. Often the additional commentary explains what the play means or why something in the play is significant or not. This "instant replay" affords one the luxury of seeing (or hearing) the action in isolation from all other activity. This insulated look provides an opportunity to monitor the activity quite differently than the self-monitoring one can do in the heat of the action. It provides that "second look" to pick up on the subtleties and nuances missed the first time.

In the classroom example, of course, the "instant replay" differs slightly from high-tech television. The classroom "replay" is played back without the announcer's commentary. However, the teacher or a peer can provide valuable and insightful comments, and students who are featured on the tape can give comments as well.

"Instant replay" is a viable monitoring device in this age of ever-increasing technology because both audio recorders and video recorders are readily available in most schools. In addition, the students of today, no matter how young, are comfortable with that technology. They use it with ease and appreciate its renderings, probably far more than many of the adults in their world, who are more "gun shy" about hi-tech innovations.

Yet, once teachers begin to use this concept of "instant replay," they become adept with the uses of the various pieces of equipment. And, the "replay" becomes such a valuable self-assessment tool that whatever challenges there are in using technology, they are easily overridden by the benefits.

TAPE RECORDINGS

hy Although the use of recording in analyzing human behavior is well documented in the literature on educational psychology and cognitive psychology, and videotaping and audiotaping are commonplace in schools, the "instant replay" technique is perhaps not as widely used. However, for students to be able to see or hear themselves, to have that second look, almost immediately, is a potent tool in helping them become more skillful in their metacognitive reflections.

Feuerstein and others clearly demonstrate the modifiability of the cognitive processes through deliberate and systematic interventions. "Instant replay" might be construed as a mediation strategy. The "instant replay" provides a ready-made tape to review as students learn to monitor their own learning. As Feuerstein says, "students must learn how to learn." By playing back tapes of the dialogues, conversations, and articulations, they are privy to examine, analyze, and evaluate their just-finished interactions. The learning episode is extended, expanded, and extrapolated through the "instant replay" and the accompanying monologue or dialogue.

———————————◆———————————

How The idea of the "instant replay" as a monitoring strategy is sparked by the work of a young teacher in British Columbia. Immersed in an environment rich with materials for hands-on learning, the children have at their disposal small, hand-held tape recorders (the type one typically takes to a meeting or seminar). In this busy classroom of projects and investigative learning, they are encouraged to tape their conversations as they work in partners or small groups so the teacher can later play the tapes and/or share them with the children as they evaluate the learning episodes.

If recorded conversations are viable assessment tools that help teachers and students evaluate learning, it seems to follow that these same recordings might be valuable monitoring

TAPE RECORDINGS

tools to use immediately after the dialogue takes place. Rather than waiting to assess what is on the tapes, why not make the recording an integral part of the learning episode. Let students record their questions, comments, and ideas as they investigate, experiment, and "mess around" with an idea or problem. Then, within the same time interval, have them incorporate an "instant replay" of the tape to help them understand what occurred.

While students use the "instant replay," the teacher may listen to or view the tape with the students involved and model questions and comments that monitor the activity taped. For example, the teacher might say, "I noticed you both said it looked larger. Do you still agree?" or "There seems to be a lot of talking and confusion about what you observed during the lab experiment from the instant replay. Pick out the most important observation that was made."

After some modeling by the teacher and repeated guided practice, students are then able to monitor their own "instant replay" as part of the activity. Within a fairly short time, students become quite sophisticated with this technique and use it throughout their investigations. Teachers report hearing students say, "Let's play that back. Maybe we missed something important because it happened so fast and we were so excited."

Of course, the use of the "instant replay" does not preclude the use of the taped data as a self-assessment tool in evaluating metacognitively.

When Early in the process of teaching students to be more metacognitive, one looks for scaffolds to help the learner understand. It seems that in this particular strategy, the use of "instant replays" with audio- or videotaped recordings offers the learner just that physical crutch to lean on to become better at monitoring their thinking through their dialogue and/or visual actions. The appropriate opportunities for use are many.

TAPE RECORDINGS

"Instant replay" seems appropriate for all age groups since the seeds of the strategy are planted in the early childhood classroom, and the use of tape decks and camcorders by teens is a well-known phenomena. In fact, even adult learners are likely candidates for the "instant replay" strategy as they monitor their interactions in learning experiences.

More specifically, "instant replay" might be introduced through an all-class interaction. As the teacher and students brainstorm ideas on the board about earthquakes, a tape recording of the process can be made. Immediately following the actual brainstorm, the tape is played back as students answer the questions,

"What did we do well in the brainstorm?"
and
"What might we do differently another time?"

Following this introductory example, and a teacher commentary on what has just happened with the "instant replay," the students can begin to tape their conversations during science investigations or during a library search. Then, with the playback or instant replay, they assess their work and gain insight into their learning.

One Idea

 Tape discussions between partners or cooperative groups who are working on a thought-provoking project or lab assignment. After students have completed the assignment, they play back their discussions, examining their solution paths and their thinking. Students discuss how "instant replay" helps them to understand how they arrived at their solutions. Ask these questions to spark their reflection:

How did the "instant replay" help or hinder you?

Would you like to use it again? Why?

Where else do you think this method would be helpful?

My Idea

Jot down one idea for this metacognitive tool.

_____

_____

_____

_____

_____

_____

_____

_____

_____

_____

_____

_____

_____

_____

_____

_____

My Reflection

What I Did

Log your use of the idea. Explain what you actually did, giving some details but mostly just the "big idea."

_____

_____

_____

_____

_____

_____

_____

_____

_____

_____

_____

_____

_____

What I Think

Reflect on the activity. What are the pluses and minuses? What other thoughts do you have?

_____

_____

_____

_____

_____

_____

_____

_____

_____

_____

_____

_____

_____

Afterthoughts

STRATEGY 5

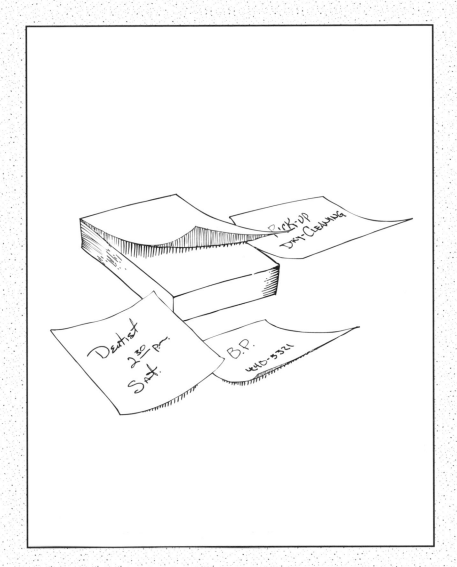

Post-it Note

[MEMOING]

MEMOING

Memoing is an extension of the written reminders on yellow Post-it notecards saying, "Don't forget to feed the cat." "These dishes are dirty." or "Dentist, 4:30, Monday!" Memoing is a sophisticated technique of reviewing pieces of work and jotting down generalizations or specifications that refer to the original work. Memoing is taking time to comment on a previously completed work in order to provide insight or elaboration to the idea. The memo often takes the form of a commentary that makes some relevant observation about the idea. For example, in scripting a videotape, the scriptwriter actually records the action and dialogue on the tape. However, if that writer also makes comments along the side of the script, that is called memoing. For example, the writer may make notes next to the script that signal an important part or a place to stop and intervene with an activity. Memoing provides the metacognitive comment, the running monologue.

Memoing is similar to an editorial comment or a parenthetical phrase that occurs as one reviews material. At this stage, the learner metaphorically stands outside, looking in at the original piece, in order to provide additional comments that illuminate the original idea.

In fact, memoing can also be linked to the stage directions written in italics in a play. While the dialogue provides the ongoing, rapid-fire conversation, the stage directions, sequenced intermittently, give additional needed directions to the actors. Memoing, just like the stage directions, provides similar instructive information for the learner with cues in the script at appropriate spots.

Miles and Huberman (1984) elaborate on the technique of memoing in their book on qualitative analysis. They promote the strategy of memoing as a monitoring and management tool for the volumes of observational notes that accumulate in a systematic descriptive study. The intermittent memoing technique keeps the researcher constantly reviewing the mass of material and making sense of the multitude of observational data. Memoing also helps make

MEMOING

the notes more manageable when the memo takes on the form of coding. A memo code signals the researcher about the type of observation, a category of sorts, for the voluminous notes. For example, a classroom researcher might code all open-ended teacher questions as OET and all open-ended student questions as OES.

Inherent in this strategy is an idea that Glaser (1965) also uses in his constant comparative methodology for analyzing qualitative data. By constantly reviewing what is there, one is forced to look again at the idea, and, of course, in that second look, the mind makes new and different connections. In the afterthought, this extraneous information often provides insightful understanding.

While the roots of this strategy stretch back into "heavy duty" research methodology, the strategy is really quite friendly for student use. In fact, it is similar to the commonly heard instructions that teachers give to "reread your writing; revise your draft; make necessary changes." The only difference is that rather than revamping the original work, memoing requires a more contemplative note of why the particular part is flagged as significant or how it connects to key ideas. As a classroom technique, memoing fosters monitoring strategies for students while they are actually working with the material.

How To teach students to memo as a metacognitive monitoring strategy, begin with the most viable of all teaching techniques—modeling. Teachers can actually show students how to use memoing, for example, in their lab notes. As students record their procedures and observations, the teacher can move from team to team and actually read the entries and make a memo along the side to model what memoing is. Or, this can be more expediently done on a transparency to demonstrate the process. In either case, this is simply the introductory piece to show students the actual idea of memoing.

After this brief awareness lesson, students can be required to make a memo in the margin of every lab entry. For example, as they study about genetic traits in the biology lab, they may note that their observations in the lab examples resemble their personal experience. Or

MEMOING

they may make a running commentary throughout their labs on how each investigation relates to the theory of evolution. This latter example may take the form of coding or categorizing their written records.

With young children, the memoing technique may be more often verbal than written. This can be facilitated by the teacher's questions, leading students to draw some conclusion, make some inferences, or even develop a generalization about an activity. Even if the whole group contributes to a "chart story" about turtles, questioning can guide the memoing of ideas. For example, students might conclude that they know a lot about turtles, but not much about baby turtles. The teacher can then make a memo on their chart to that effect.

The memo facilitates more in-depth thinking about the topic. It focuses the student on learning about two aspects of things. In the first, how the genetic theory relates to them personally, and in the second example, they now have some direction for further study—finding out more about baby turtles.

In summary, memoing is a process that calls for a thorough look at the material while one is still in the act of working with it. The memo enhances the observation; it provides that metacognitive note that is so important in facilitating meaningful transfer of learning.

When Without repeating the above, the most opportune time to use memoing is when students are furiously recording their observations during an instructional activity. It is in their flurry of activity that students most need a moment to stop and think about what it is they are doing and learning. Memoing is a deliberate intervention that requires extrapolation and generalization—the very skills inherent in the transfer process.

Eventually, students understand the power of the memoed notes and initiate their use on their own. They see that the connections that are made are the key, umbrella ideas that help them remember and understand what is important. These memos become the threads that weave through the learning and provide common chunks or big ideas for easy assimilations.

One Idea

 Encourage students to use the memoing technique when watching a movie or filmstrip in class. You can even pause the activity to allow them ample time to react and write about what they are viewing. After viewing the piece, discuss the content as well as the memoed notes students have recorded.

Use the memoing strategy in the writing process as well. As students write their first drafts, have them take time to think about their writing. In the margins, they can record their reactions and thoughts. During the next phase of writing, they can pay attention to their memoed notes and take them into consideration when revising.

My Idea

Jot down one idea for this metacognitive tool.

_____

_____

_____

_____

_____

_____

_____

_____

_____

_____

_____

_____

_____

_____

_____

My Reflection

What I Did

Log your use of the idea. Explain what you actually did, giving some details but mostly just the "big idea."

_____

_____

_____

_____

_____

_____

_____

_____

_____

_____

_____

_____

_____

What I Think

Reflect on the activity. What are the pluses and minuses? What other thoughts do you have?

_____

_____

_____

_____

_____

_____

_____

_____

_____

_____

_____

_____

_____

Afterthoughts

STRATEGY 6

Le Menu

Mental Menus

[TRACKING]

TRACKING

Mnemonic devices have been a part of the classroom instructional repertoire, it seems, since time began. Remember the little ditty to help recall how to spell Mississippi: "*M*, *I*, crooked letter, crooked letter, *I*, crooked letter, crooked letter, *I*, hump back, hump back, *I*." Or think back to the rhyme, "I before E except after C . . ."; or the reminder for how to divide fractions; "Yours is not to reason why, just invert and multiply."

Many of these mnemonic devices take the form of acronyms, such as in music. FACE stands for each note on the spaces of the music staff. HOMES is a way to remember the five names of the Great Lakes: Huron, Ontario, Michigan, Erie, and Superior.

Mental menus are much like these familiar and readily recalled mnemonics that are used extensively by some learners. These mental steps to problem solving serve as a mental menu, spelling out the word IDEA.

Identify the problem.

Develop alternatives.

Execute a solution.

Assess the results.

This mental menu gives students a standard set of procedures to return to or to review as they approach problems in and across the various disciplines. Mental menus are internal cue cards that signal a path of operation. Just as the cue card prompts the actor on stage in a momentary lapse of memory, the mental cue card prompts the learner with a reliable set of instructions. Mental menus are often used with the teaching of thinking skills. For example, in teaching prediction as a creative skill that requires the learner to project beyond the given information, the acronym BET is used.

B = **B**ase your bet on the best information you have.

E = **E**xpress possibilities and probabilities in your search for ideas.

T = **T**ender your bet by making an educated guess or a prediction.

In addition, mental menus are common in procedures that are to be used over and over again. An illustration that is familiar to all is the computer in which the mental menu be-

TRACKING

comes a visual reality. The menu of operations in this example can actually be called up any time the user chooses to review options; so, too, in the mental menus monitoring strategy. As a metacognitive tool, the menu can be called to mind by the user to aid in the execution of a given activity. Each time one is expected to make a prediction, the mental menu, BET can be recalled, restated, and reviewed as a tool in arriving at a thoughtful prediction.

Why The research suggests that mental menus are useful cognitive tools. For instance, de Bono's (1983) use of the mental menu in advancing the idea of the explicit instruction in thinking skills is well known in the field. The PMI strategy of Plus, Minus, and Interesting is commonplace in the thinking classroom. Actually, de Bono presents sixty separate menus in the complete program. Others that one easily remembers are the OPV, (Other Point of View) and the AGO (Aims, Goals, and Objectives) and PO (Possibility Thinking).

Along the same line, Ogle's (1986) KWL (What do we **Know**; **Want** to know, and what have we **Learned**) is a well-used mental menu in the whole language classroom. The KWL menu cues students to think about prior knowledge, anticipate what is intriguing and evaluate what they learn—all viable metacognitive strategies for learning about our learning.

The power of mental menus and other mnemonic devices is also hailed by others in the literature working within the cognitive area of memory. Guilford's (1975) Structure of the Intellect model (SOI), stresses five cognitive realms in which to stimulate intellectual activity: cognition, evaluation, divergent production, convergent production, and memory. Within that cognitive model, Meeker (1976) has developed a set of tasks that draw on the concept of creating mental menus.

Another literary source who reports positive results with the use of mental menus is Lorayne in *The Memory Book* (1974). In addition, Fogarty and Bellanca present twenty-four thinking skills with mental menus, in their early piece, *Teach Them Thinking: Mental Menus for 24 Thinking Skills* (1986). And, of course, one must mention again, the obvious use of menus—the Apple computer software programs.

TRACKING

How

These mental cue cards or mental menus can be developed by the teacher, the class as a whole, or the students themselves as they work with an idea. In order to develop the use of mental menus, rampant and explicit use of them in the classroom is mandatory. In fact, the posting of the menu on charts may mentally precipitate the acquisition of it for the students. For example, the acronym for the writing process reminds students about the various steps to follow:

Write a first draft.

Revise the draft.

Insist on an outside critique.

Test, by reading aloud.

Enter the final version for publishing.

After working with mental menus explicitly and repeatedly in the classroom, the process eventually becomes an indelible mental chart for the students. Once the writing process is internalized, it can be called up mentally, throughout the extended process of writing a finished piece. In this way, it acts as a self-monitoring device that is always available for the students to use.

Of course, mental menus are often much less formalized, created at will by the learner as a set of mental procedures that is needed. For example, it may be as simple as a trick for remembering the combination to a lock.

Sometimes, however, the mental menu acts as a trigger for a more complex series of operations. "Touch Down, P.F.C." is one that comes to mind. It is a homemade reminder of the findings of Joyce and Showers (1980) regarding the critical elements of teacher training:

Touch	=	Theory
Down	=	Demonstration
Private	=	Practice
First	=	Feedback
Class	=	Coaching

TRACKING

Touch Down, P.F.C. is easy to remember. And, with a bit of mindful attention, one is able to transfer the mental cue cards back into the original concepts. Somehow that simple cue triggers the mind to recover the original learning. The mental menu acts like a real menu—by previewing the entrée to come.

———————◆———————

hen The informal introduction of mental menus is ongoing, beginning almost serendipitously early in the students' school career. Teachers can utilize them throughout the curriculum. Yet, a more formal introduction is recommended as the focus on self-regulating metacognitive strategies becomes part of the students' cognitive development. Perhaps at some point in a lesson in which students are expected to know a set of facts or grasp a procedure, an acronym can be modeled by the teacher. In this introduction, students merely memorize or internalize the mental menu.

After doing that modeling a few times, the teacher can then ask small groups to develop a menu for another learning episode. Using the creative input of the team members, groups easily develop quite usable mental menus.

Finally, when the time seems right and students have had time to play with the idea of creating mental menus, they are asked to develop one on their own—or maybe in partners. Once they have experienced mental menu cues in this way, they continue to use them because they prove to be helpful.

Again, this can be initiated at any age since students seem to use metacognitive reflection at fairly early ages. It also seems appropriate to demonstrate the use of mental menus as opportunities arise during focus activities. The use of mental menus is an integral and continuous part of the learning as students learn to rely on the menus as they mentally monitor their learning episodes.

One Idea

 To introduce your students to mental menus, explain the mnemonic devices and acronyms discussed in this chapter, such as HOMES (the Great Lakes), IDEA (ways to problem solve), WRITE (the steps in the writing process), and BET (the strategy for making a prediction). Do not overload them; simply show them that some key words and phrases can help them recall more complicated processes and information. Also, introduce students to the acronym ROY G. BIV—as someone's name that stands for the colors in the spectrum.

Red
Orange
Yellow
Green
Blue
Indigo
Violet

To build awareness of these devices, start a bulletin board or class book in which students collect and record these mental menus from all sources. Students can ask parents, relatives, siblings, teachers, neighbors—anyone that they can think of about types of mental menus they use to help them remember things. Once this project is complete, review as a class all of the information collected. Of course students are not expected to remember all of them. However, there will be some they adapt for their own use. Once students are comfortable with mental menus, they can use them in class and create their own.

My Idea

Jot down one idea for this metacognitive tool.

_____

_____

_____

_____

_____

_____

_____

_____

_____

_____

_____

_____

_____

_____

_____

_____

My Reflection

What I Did

Log your use of the idea. Explain what you actually did, giving some details but mostly just the "big idea."

_____

_____

_____

_____

_____

_____

_____

_____

_____

_____

_____

_____

_____

What I Think

Reflect on the activity. What are the pluses and minuses? What other thoughts do you have?

_____

_____

_____

_____

_____

_____

_____

_____

_____

_____

_____

_____

_____

Afterthoughts

STRATEGY 7

Cue Cards

[PROMPTING]

PROMPTING

**What** Cues are recognizable and predetermined signals that alert the learner to think about what is going on. Cues are deliberate, verbal, or visual prompts that perform the same function as the understudy or teleprompter in a dramatic production. However, in the classroom, cues take on many forms, from the key question posed by the teacher in the midst of an investigation to actual cards and/or charts displayed at the appropriate, teachable moment. These verbal cues and written prompts only slightly interrupt the flow of cognitive activity as students step back for a moment to think in a more metacognitive way.

For example, in the middle of small group brainstorms in which students are creating a fluent listing of ideas for their research reports in global studies, the teacher interrupts the activity with a cueing question: "Which are the broad topics and which topics seem more narrow?" By cueing this evaluative categorization during the activity, the teacher fosters metacognitive monitoring of the types of topics being generated. And, just by cueing students to this idea of broad and narrow topics, they implicitly begin to label their ideas in that way.

A written cue, on the other hand, might simply take the form of the teacher walking about the classroom, flashing a sign to each small group signaling them to "Select three ideas that are personally relevant," or jotting down a time reminds, "five minutes!" This metacognitive cueing prompts students toward personal involvement rather than merely continuing in the think-tank mode of generating many ideas.

Cues are natural monitors that many teachers already use. It's just a matter of identifying the cueing technique so teachers can become more skillful in its use.

———◆———

**Why** Cueing or prompting students to shift from the cognitive to the metacognitive is a strategy in Beyer's (1987) work on explicit thinking skills instruction in which cueing is employed to alert students to use a particular type of thinking skill. Beyer suggests the use of cues is critical to the early instruction and guided practice stages. For example, Beyer points out to

PROMPTING

students who have classified a group of vocabulary words that through the process of labeling and sorting, they have gleaned some insight into the text from which the words were taken. In doing this, he deliberately cues their predicting abilities to set the stage for reading.

Also, supporting evidence for the idea of cueing strategies is found in Perkins' work, *Knowledge as Design* (1986). In the context of thinking within a design or a super-imposed framework, Perkins uses cues to guide student thinking and to scaffold transfer. He suggests four questions about its purpose, structure, model cases, and arguments that explain and evaluate it. To illustrate Perkins' use of cues, students working on an idea are prompted to think about how the idea might be useful in another context; how the idea might be transferred or applied in other circumstances—either in academic subjects or in life.

Cueing is a method of metacognitive prompts or guideposts that point the way toward deeper and more meaningful learning. The consistent use of cueing facilitates student-initiated use of their own mental cueing later on. It is a fairly easy strategy to incorporate once teachers begin to focus on metacognitive reflection.

How Spontaneous, appropriate use of cueing and prompting is an easy way to start the process of getting students to respond to mental cues. By demonstrating with explicit cues, such as asking students to note why they are doing a particular task, students begin to tune in to that "little voice inside their head" that beckons to them with mental cues and prompts. For example, once students are aware of their own internal self-monitoring cues, they are more likely to take heed when that mental voice says, "Don't forget to frame the story for events in the news. It's supposed to present a current controversy." or "Find the known, then, proceed to the unknown." Cueing is taught, first explicitly, in somewhat formal lessons. As Feuerstein (1980) instructs in his *Instrumental Enrichment* program, the students must be equipped with a precise cognitive vocabulary before they are able to articulate properly about their thinking. They need to know specific vocabulary and to practice using that vocabulary to describe their thinking processes.

PROMPTING

Then, once they have a grasp of the words that explain their mental behaviors, they are able to become more skillful in tracking their thinking. Mental cueing and mental prompting are ideas that they experience already, even at very young ages. Children are aware of a superordinate kind of thinking that goes on in their heads—aside from the focus thought. Once they can identify it in words, they use it in their metacognitive conversations.

———————◆———————

When Cueing is most effective when used during the various activities structured to explicitly enhance student thinking. Opportune times in the primary classroom to use cueing strategies to monitor student thinking occur often during discussion time. When students are reacting to teacher-directed activities, the teacher can easily cue them to think more metacognitively by calling their attention to a point of reflection. For example, the teacher may suggest in the midst of a discussion on *friendship*, to take a moment to tell a partner about being a good friend; why it is sometimes difficult; when it is easy. This takes the concept of friendship from a topic to be studied, to a relevant discussion about their own behavior. It makes them more aware of how they act as a friend. It cues thinking about their own actions.

On the other hand, in the upper-level classes, student partners can be instructed into ways to cue each other in dialogues about their work. For example, the peer writing conference is a perfect opportunity for this metacognitive monitoring. As the writer reads his/her piece, the listener not only critiques the writing for grammatical errors or awkward language, but prompts the writer to reflect on what he or she is trying to convey in tone, pacing, or direction of plot. This cueing helps the author pay attention to the metacognitive considerations that may otherwise get lost in the concern over technical correctness.

Cueing or prompting as a metacognitive monitoring tool tends to take on the characteristics of a snowball. It grows and develops more rapidly than at first expected. As cueing takes shape, just like the embryonic snowball, it suddenly picks up a momentum of its own. At the more advanced stages, cueing is obvious throughout the classroom: teachers cue students, students cue each other, and eventually, students mentally cue themselves to stand aside and think metacognitively for a moment.

One Idea

 Discuss the concept of using cues as reminders for encouraging students to stop and reflect on a topic. Give examples of opportunities where students can use the cueing strategy. Have students practice this strategy during a reading or literature lesson.

For elementary students, practice cueing in a teacher-directed activity such as reading a story aloud to them. Stop briefly throughout the story to cue them. Have them consider motives for the actions of various characters, the consequences of the characters' actions, and what may happen next. Have them think about these ideas as they listen to the rest of the story.

After completing the story, ask students to give feedback on the cueing strategy itself. Does stopping to think about the characters and plot help them to understand the story better or worse? Why? What kinds of things do they think about? Have students practice the cueing strategy themselves with any subject, just by asking themselves questions in their heads. Provide additional guided practice, by having students pick a short story of their own and work with a partner to jot down questions they asked themselves as they read.

With older students, use the cueing technique during a science lecture, during a class discussion, or while students are working with partners in the lab. Throughout the lesson stop and give cues for students to think about what they are doing and what types of cause and effect relationships are present. Ask partners to record the cues and responses they give each other. After the lesson or lab is completed, discuss how the cues help or hinder the science lesson. Does cueing lead anyone to think differently? Does it raise any questions or new ideas? Discuss what types of cues students could give themselves if they are working alone in another subject. How could this thinking skill carry over into other areas?

My Idea

Jot down one idea for this metacognitive tool.

_____

_____

_____

_____

_____

_____

_____

_____

_____

_____

_____

_____

_____

My Reflection

What I Did

Log your use of the idea. Explain what you actually did, giving some details but mostly just the "big idea."

_____

_____

_____

_____

_____

_____

_____

_____

_____

_____

_____

_____

_____

What I Think

Reflect on the activity. What are the pluses and minuses? What other thoughts do you have?

_____

_____

_____

_____

_____

_____

_____

_____

_____

_____

_____

_____

_____

Afterthoughts

STRATEGY 8

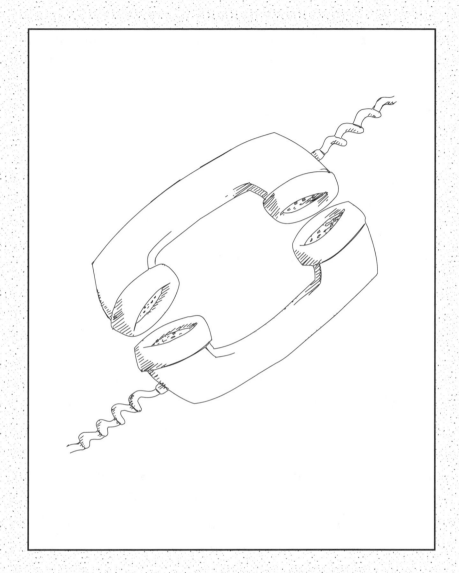

Two-Way Talk

[CONFERENCING]

CONFERENCING

Conferencing is usually considered an evaluation strategy in which the teacher meets with the parents and shares information about a student's progress. Or, in light of the focus today on authentic assessment, conferencing can also be a student-led conference in which the student takes the lead in sharing his or her portfolio of work with the parents and teacher, explaining why certain selections were made. However, the conferencing targeted here is a formative strategy that is ongoing, sometimes spontaneous, and always a two-way interaction between the student and a peer, teacher, or team of cohorts.

Conferencing is a face-to-face interaction that yields a reflection on the project at hand. It is a technique for soliciting one-on-one feedback—a personal, verbal transaction that focuses on the why and how of something, not the what, who, when, and where of that something.

For example, students of all ages frequently use conferencing in the writing process. After completing a first draft, the author meets with a peer and reads his or her piece aloud and then conferences with the partner, asking questions, answering questions, and genuinely "kicking around" ideas about how to improve the original draft.

Another example of conferencing, common in classrooms across the country, is a goal-setting conference in which students dialogue with each other in order to set reasonable goals in a particular class. One such conference involves high school students in physical education, setting goals about their health and fitness for a specific quarter. Based on knowledge about their own state of fitness in areas such as agility, fat content, strength, endurance, and flexibility, students conference with peers and, of course, their instructors to gain insight into realistic and achievable goals. This conferencing technique continues throughout the quarter, monitoring progress and making necessary adjustments.

Conferencing is a natural monitoring strategy. Just as therapists monitor patient medication, behavior, and overall mental stability through intermittent conferencing, the classroom that mirrors a philosophy of self-regulatory, developmental learning, also uses conferencing to periodically check on the state of things.

Conferencing is simply the act of talking with another person in order to reflectively mediate one's activity or behavior. The conferencing technique highlighted here is informal, frequent, and ongoing. It is an integral part of the interactive classroom of active learners.

CONFERENCING

Although the proponents of cooperative learning do not use the term conferencing explicitly, the literature in this area is steeped in rationalization and confirmation of the positive outcomes of the verbal articulation that occurs in group work. Johnson and Johnson (1987), Kagan (1992), Slavin (1983), and Bellanca and Fogarty (1991) all support the concept of verbal interaction through formalized cooperative learning groups as conducive to more meaningful learning. Through the process of putting ideas into words and trying to dialogue with others and clarify ideas, students internalize concepts in deeper, more substantive ways.

Thus, it follows that the conferencing technique, used to metacognitively monitor one's thinking and ideas, is a viable strategy to encourage in the cooperative/cognitive classroom. Conferencing, or person-to-person interaction, is not only an expedient classroom strategy to track student thinking, but it is also one that students enjoy immensely, regardless of their age. Kids love to talk to each other.

The rationale for conferencing seems simple and straightforward; to talk through ideas with other interested parties is as old as Socrates. Socratic dialogue relies on the skillful interaction between two people to reveal fallacies in reasoning and gaps in logic. The positive results of this kind of dialogue is well-respected in the field and has been the catalyst for many high-level philosophical discussions that lead to greater self-awareness.

How Role playing and staged conferencing simulations are both effective ways to teach this monitoring strategy to students. The conferencing strategy can, at first, be carefully scripted to illustrate the "give and take" of a productive conference. Probing questions that paraphrase, clarify, and affirm can be modeled and exaggerated to make a point: *Specifically, what do you mean? In other words. . . , I agree. . . .* Later, or in another situation, the conferencing

CONFERENCING

dialogue can be more spontaneous and less preplanned. However, both conferencing lessons can simulate the key elements of a good conference. These critical components include:

Selecting a partner.
Finding an appropriate time and place.
Preparing for a good conference.
Responding appropriately.
Determining desired outcomes.

However, the role plays or simulations are probably more powerful teaching tools in themselves, without overdoing the explicit instruction about what must or must not be included in conferencing. It seems more appropriate to demonstrate the naturalness of talking things over with another person. As the saying goes, "Two heads are better than one."

Another technique for teaching students about conferencing is to videotape or audiotape actual student conferences and then play back the tapes in a teacher-student conference so that both can react, give feedback, and critique the conferencing episode. This strategy is usually quite motivating for the students as most like to be audiotaped and videotaped. It gives them that second look—a chance to refine their conferencing skills. Also, the recordings allow students to hear both their comments and questions and the responses of the conferencing partner in a more relaxed setting. By reviewing the whole conversation, they learn how to improve when they are in the speaking role in a conference and when they are in the listening role.

Since humans have naturally sought counsel by talking things over with their "peers" and their "elders" since time began, it is logical to assume that conferencing is a strategy that is easily embraced by the students. With a single demonstration, students are sufficiently prepared to employ this monitoring technique. Conferencing is just one more tool for students to metacognitively reflect on their development, but it is one that will continue throughout their lives. For it is natural to want to "bounce ideas" off another person. This strategy formalizes that process of seeking counsel.

CONFERENCING

hen The conferencing technique is probably best used after students have gotten to know each other, rather than too early in the semester when they are still feeling a bit unsure of themselves. In fact, it is a good idea to facilitate the strategy by letting students choose their conferencing partners, at least in the beginning, because trust plays a significant part in effective conferencing. When there is a noticeable level of trust, students are more likely to be honest and fair in their feedback. If the trust is lacking, two things can happen: (1) the critique may be sugar-coated in order to not hurt anyone's feelings or (2) the feedback may be brutally honest and then one risks a backlash or defensive retort. In either case, the conferencing has not resulted in the desired outcome, which is to solicit helpful comments that focus on improvement.

However, once students are familiar with conferencing and feel comfortable asking various classmates to participate in a conference with them, the strategy can be utilized frequently and informally. It simply becomes another way for students to monitor, reflect, and solicit feedback on their work in progress.

The conferencing may take the form of a group conference or a teacher/student conference. While student-to-student conferences are often the easiest to facilitate in the classroom and the most popular with the students themselves, the other models offer several new options. The group conference offers multiple perspectives on an idea and the teacher/student conference offers the "expert opinion" versus the peer opinion. Depending on the purpose of the conference and the stage of the project, the various conference options are taken under consideration.

One Idea

 Integrate the technique of conferencing with writing skills and a content area in science. Middle and high school students can select any lab report that they have written recently as the subject of their conference. Each student works with a partner with whom he or she practices conferencing skills and each pair is videotaped. The goal is to build their skills in critiquing each other's work with thoughtful comments and criticisms. Students can provide valuable feedback for improving the content of the lab reports.

Each pair takes turns playing the role of scientist and researcher. In the scientist's role, the student is expected to critique the researcher's lab report for content, specifically paying attention to the explanation and observations made during the experiment. Scientists should encourage the researchers to focus on the "why" and "how" of the experiment and offer suggestions for improvement. Researchers can ask questions and discuss their own thoughts on the lab report as well. After the conference is complete, students switch roles so that each has a chance to discuss. Students then rewrite their lab reports based on the results of their conference.

My Idea

Jot down one idea for this metacognitive tool.

_____

_____

_____

_____

_____

_____

_____

_____

_____

_____

_____

_____

_____

_____

_____

_____

My Reflection

What I Did

Log your use of the idea. Explain what you actually did, giving some details but mostly just the "big idea."

_____

_____

_____

_____

_____

_____

_____

_____

_____

_____

_____

_____

_____

What I Think

Reflect on the activity. What are the pluses and minuses? What other thoughts do you have?

_____

_____

_____

_____

_____

_____

_____

_____

_____

_____

_____

_____

_____

Afterthoughts

STRATEGY 9

Transfer Talk

[BRIDGING]

BRIDGING

**hat**

One of the simplest and surest ways to ensure the transfer of learning from one context to another is through "transfer talk." Transfer talk is a metacognitive message about how an idea might be used in another context; how learning can be applied in novel situations; or how inert knowledge is leveraged into meaningful transfer and subsequent use.

This metacognitive message is a deliberate reference about the targeted learning and its apparent usefulness to the learner. Transfer talk is an explicit monologue or dialogue about taking the learning from one place to another. Transfer talk cues the learner to possibilities and potential transfer opportunities. Like a bridge for learning, transfer talk connects one learning situation to another. Similarly, both the constructed bridge and the cognitive bridge vary in style, length, and elaboration.

Sometimes, the transfer talk is very short: "Learning the keyboard will help you with your word processing skills." Other times, the bridge spans a wider gap between the original learning and its use in another area: "Learning a foreign language will be useful when you travel abroad." And, in some cases, the bridge is so long its anchor point is a bit obscure: "Learning about the human body will give you insight into other closed systems."

However, transfer talk is the bridging technique that helps students recognize the usefulness of their learning. It is clearly a necessary metacognitive message system that promotes active learning as well as relevant learning. In fact, by deliberately focusing student attention on the application stage of learning through frequent transfer talk in the classroom, teachers move students beyond the mere recall of facts and into higher levels of thinking and metacognition. Thus, both the cognitive and metacognitive realms are stimulated in the minds of the learners.

———————————— ◆ ————————————

**hy**

The reasons for wanting to facilitate transfer are obvious. Without meaningful application, much of what students learn would remain as inert knowledge, simply gathered and stored. On the other hand, when students become aware of relevant uses for things they learn, that learning becomes more engaging because of the anticipated useful outcomes.

BRIDGING

While the need for transfer is well documented in the literature, probably the most well-known and respected voice in the field on mediation strategies is Feuerstein's (1980) work on metacognition. Throughout his authored material on cognitive modifiability, he demonstrates intervention strategies that stress mediation that is accompanied by continuous and consistent talk about transfer and use in other situations beyond the initial learning episodes.

In addition, Perkins and Salomon (1988) approach the concept of transfer talk in their work on transfer. They distinguish between "near" transfer and "far" transfer and suggest that "far" or remote transfer is fostered by making mindful abstractions. It follows that mindful abstractions may take the form of articulating the connections or talking about transfer.

Fogarty (1989) also addresses the transfer issue in the context of teacher trainings and concludes that by attending to transfer and making learners aware of their levels of transfer through explicit dialogue, transfer is quite easily increased. In fact, teachers are coached in the levels of transfer—overlooking, duplicating, replicating, integrating, mapping, and innovating—and are encouraged to dialogue in peer partners about their transfer.

In addition, Fogarty, Perkins, and Barell (1992) develop a set of strategies that promote both the simple, almost automatic kind of transfer and the more complex or remote transfer that requires mediation. All agree that transfer must be explicitly discussed—the strategy of "transfer talk."

How

In its most crystallized form, the teacher uses transfer talk by suggesting possible transfer ideas. He or she simply states likely applications. For example, while working with fractions, the teacher deliberately points out the usefulness of fractions in following recipes and in measuring the lengths of a room for carpeting. This simpler transfer talk alerts students to relevant applications.

Another example of transfer talk is in teacher-questioning techniques. Rather than telling students the possibilities for further use of an idea, in this illustration the teacher elicits ideas from the students with transfer talk that takes the form of probing questions:

BRIDGING

How might you use this?

When have you used this before?

How can you describe a new application?

Why are you learning this?

How is this idea relevant?

In addition to the teacher directly engaging in the transfer talk or facilitating questions for students to target likely transfer situations, transfer talk can also be fostered in student-to-student interactions. For instance, while working in the lab on the various states of matter, science students are directed to dialogue about the usefulness of the concept of changing solids to liquids or gases. Of course, what follows is somewhat awkward conversation about how what they are learning is possibly going to be of any use to them outside the science lab. This transfer talk leads students to look for connections from "book learning" and the "practical world." And, in their search for meaning through this metacognitive dialogue, students become aware of the transfer.

While transfer talk requires extremely high-level thinking and promotes complex cognitive activity, it is a strategy that can be utilized fairly easily in all classroom situations, for it takes very little time. The critical element is only that the teacher pay attention to the idea of transfer by either talking about it personally or getting the students to engage in talk about relevant learning as an integral part of any lesson.

Once teachers begin to consistently use transfer talk and constantly cue students to potentials for transfer, it is a natural outcome that students soon begin to initiate transfer talk on their own. Transfer talk really answers student queries about, "Why am I learning this?" or "Am I ever gonna use this again?" because they naturally punctuate their learning with references to future uses or possible transfer opportunities.

While this idea seems so simple and such a natural part of the learning process, it is surprising to note that transfer really does not get the amount of explicit attention we think it does. In fact, transfer has been so neglected historically, Perkins (1992) refers to transfer in his Bo Peep theory of transfer and his "lost sheep" idea. He suggests instead, "The Good Shepherd" theory in which transfer is shepherded. Thus, "transfer talk" becomes the shepherd.

BRIDGING

 Appropriate use of the transfer talk strategy begins, as always, with the teacher demonstrating the behavior for students. The demonstration, of course, incorporates a running monologue of the whats, whys, and hows of the transfer talk strategy for monitoring student work. For example, as the physics teacher pontificates about the Periodic Table of Elements, students are often wondering about its significance in their lives. This is where transfer talk might create the necessary bridge into the lives of students. Simply say, "Talk with your partner for a minute about the relevance of the Periodic Table of Elements to your life." In a short time, students generate many valid connections: patterns, charting information, tests, etc. After introducing the idea and continually modeling the behavior of transfer talk, teachers can use it throughout the lesson at critical points.

The strategy probably is most helpful when students are confused about the relevance of what they are studying. Yet, talk of transfer seems an important element in most instructional interactions. With that in mind, it is safe to say that teachers are not likely to overdo the use of transfer talk. Given its power as a force in fostering relevant use and mindful application, teachers can be prodded to include this strategy as often as possible if they want students to be more metacognitive in their approach to learning.

One Idea

 To help students better understand and reflect on the concept of transfer talk, simply make the idea part of each lesson you teach. During the closure of each lesson, ask students to give you an example or two of how what they learned in this lesson can be applied to novel situations. In other words, how the knowledge they have just gained can be transferred into other subject areas and into their own lives.

When introducing transfer to older students, have them become immersed in the idea by working in cooperative groups to find examples of the concept. Divide students into groups of three to five and give each group a content area such as science, math, English, social studies, or health. Challenge them to recall several topics and concepts that they have learned recently and brainstorm a comprehensive list. Next, ask them to take five of those concepts and give several examples of how these concepts apply to other areas in school, at work, and in life. Students may choose to do this with a graphic organizer such as the web. They simply draw a circle in which they place the concept, and their examples are on lines drawn out from that circle, like a spoke in a wheel. For example, a concept that they may have learned about recently in science might include the depletion of the protective layer of ozone. Some examples of how this affects them in their own lives or other areas might include: "I may have to use a higher protection of sunscreen when I am outside or not stay in the sun as long as I have in the past." "I may have to change my habits in order to help the environment." Or—"Everything man does has repercussions. We should learn to examine the consequences of our actions."

My Idea

Jot down one idea for this metacognitive tool.

_____

_____

_____

_____

_____

_____

_____

_____

_____

_____

_____

_____

_____

_____

_____

_____

_____

My Reflection

What I Did

Log your use of the idea. Explain what you actually did, giving some details but mostly just the "big idea."

_____

_____

_____

_____

_____

_____

_____

_____

_____

_____

_____

_____

_____

What I Think

Reflect on the activity. What are the pluses and minuses? What other thoughts do you have?

_____

_____

_____

_____

_____

_____

_____

_____

_____

_____

_____

_____

_____

Afterthoughts

STRATEGY 10

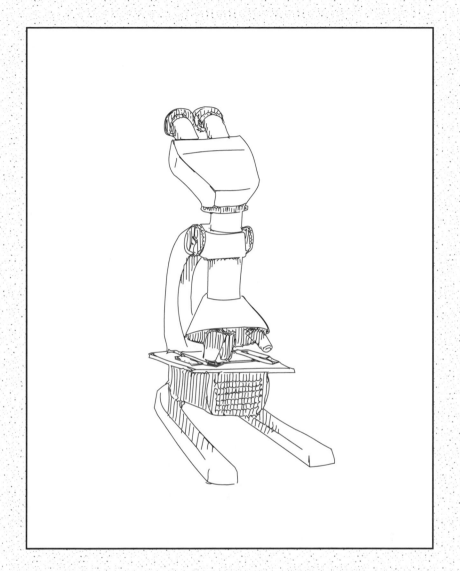

The Microscope
[RECORDED OBSERVATIONS]

RECORDED OBSERVATIONS

 While observation is an assumed technique in normative evaluation, it is sometimes undervalued as a viable monitoring tool. The learning experience can be more accurately monitored when recorded observations are part of the process.

Recorded observations are written or sketched notations made over a period of time and on a regular basis in order to extract data or extrapolate patterns of relevant information. Much like the science lab notes, recorded observations gather information that is explicitly observed, not implicitly implied. In fact, if recorded observations are to be valued as a metacognitive tool, it is during the reflection on the notes that the learner makes inferences and draws logical conclusions. But, the strategy of recording observations is just that, a permanent record of what is occurring for later analysis.

Recorded observations, unlike a log or journal, relate only the cold facts and the hard data. For example, observations can be recorded about how well the group worked in a cooperative learning situation.

A.

> Group:
> Comments:
> 1. All members were present.
> 2. Three submitted papers; one is incomplete.
> 3. Discussion lasted 20 minutes with all actively participating.

B.

	# of questions asked	#of responses	work submitted
Joey	3	1	✓
Juan	0	3	✓
Jose	4	2	0
Jill	1	2	✓

The data are then available for analysis, as illustrated by the information in Chart B.

RECORDED OBSERVATIONS

"With four members present, eight questions were asked; eight questions were answered; and three people completed the written work; it seems that the group is functioning effectively. However, one member may need clarification on the report or help in meeting deadlines."

Notice that the Chart A example also offers many specifics and provides fertile ground for making inferences and drawing conclusions. Recorded observations, whether narratives or formatted checklists, provide vital information for metacognitive reflection and self-monitoring. The key is in the content recorded: Is it fact? Is it observable? What did you see? Hear? Touch? Smell? or Taste? As Detective Friday would say on "Dragnet," "The facts, Ma'am, just the facts."

Observational data are integral parts of scientific investigations that are considered reliable and valid. Recording the facts and noting specifics epitomize empirical research and ethnographic studies. In fact, recorded observations actually drive the scientific process and lead to conclusions about the evidence.

One source that illuminates the use of recorded observations is the Miles and Huberman (1984) text on qualitative analyses. In this lengthy work, the authors illustrate myriad ways that data are recorded for comprehensive analogies. Another source that advocates recorded observation as a tool for describing the intricacies of the classroom is Eisner. In his text, *Educational Imagination*, he suggests the concept of *"connoisseurship"* in relationship to educational evaluation. *Connoisseurship* is necessary, according to Eisner, in order to fully understand and appreciate the subtleties of the classroom interactions. Only when one becomes expert as a connoisseur can one discern the differences that make something superb or ordinary; only the connoisseur carefully appreciates the complexities.

In addition to Miles and Huberman's work in qualitative analysis, as well as Eisner's, Glaser also presents evidence of the value of observational data as a viable tool for gathering needed information. In fact, Glaser's "constant comparative" methodology requires the observers to *constantly compare* their recorded notes in order to monitor the observations for pat-

RECORDED OBSERVATIONS

terns and to *constantly compare* for possible insights and conclusions as the data take shape. This continuous comparing and ongoing analysis provide many opportunities to note what is occurring, to refine and code, to reorganize and rearrange data, and to reflect and infer as ideas reoccur or as particular patterns are revisited again and again.

At one time, "scripting" was a technique to capture the entirety of teacher dialogue in the classroom in order to monitor teaching effectiveness. This observation methodology is part of Madeline Hunter's effective teaching model (1982).

Thus, while the reasons for capturing information through observational notes is well documented in the literature in both the area of qualitative research and in effective instruction, the recorded observation strategy discussed here is targeted for classroom use with students as a way to metacognitively monitor their own development.

How

To use observational notes as a monitoring tool is quite simple in today's classroom. While students are used to taking notes, they may not be as familiar with the idea of monitoring their learning through notes. So, some additions to the note-taking process are in order.

Students can be shown how to not only make notes of the information, but to also record their own, personal observations about the data. By recording observations, students actually record their impressions and reactions rather than just the traditional type of notes taken to capture information. They are trying to also capture metacognitive observations about their learning.

For example, instead of simply recording the information they are learning about the changing state of matter, they record their personal observations that relate to the phenomena of solids, liquids, and gases that they have experienced. The recorded observation is done in two steps. First, notes are made in the ordinary manner. Then, additional notes are made with personal observations, comments, reactions, insights, and emerging conclusions. This second tier of notes enhances the long-term learning for the student through the monitored observa-

RECORDED OBSERVATIONS

tions. It gently focuses the learner to deliberately take in and pay attention to the various elements that surround the learning episode. Past knowledge and prior experiences are brought to bear on the current study, as well as the momentary thoughts, ideas, and insights that occur in the heat of the action, during the actual learning process. This all-encompassing approach to note-taking, recording the circumstances that envelop the learning, as well as notes containing the actual data, constructs deep meaning within the mind of the learner.

Observational data recorded in this comprehensive manner serves as a viable study tool. Recorded observations that accompany the general note-taking strategy enrich the learning because the student is self-regulating that learning by being aware of the totality of the situation. Metacognitive monitoring is at work for the student.

While young students may not have note-taking skills that are sophisticated enough to employ this strategy as described, the teacher can certainly model it on chart paper. For example, with the whole group, the teacher can elicit both facts and observations about a video, story, or science demonstration that the children participated in. Once the facts and observations are recorded, it is quite easy to talk a bit about the differences between notes and observations, just to begin the process of recognizing both types of recorded information.

For older students, once the general note-taking strategy is operating, the teacher need only to explain the difference between notes and observations to get students thinking. Then, once they are aware of the two modes, recorded observations can be required as part of the study process. In fact, some teachers find it helpful to have the facts and data in one color and the observations in another to emphasize the differences. This color coding might be a scaffolding strategy to get them on their way.

Eventually, students automatically self-regulate by noting their observations as well as their data, because they understand the learning power when the entire episode is capsulated in notes.

One Idea

 Use observation techniques with middle and high school students studying history and sociology. Challenge students to do more than simply read their texts. Ask them to react to their books. In addition to taking notes, which consist of basic facts (i.e., dates and places where events happened), ask students to record their own observations, personal comments, reactions, insights, and feelings about what they are reading. Students may use different colored pens in order to differentiate their notes from their observations.

For example, students reading about the Boston Tea Party may record facts such as "It happened at Boston Harbor in 1773; colonists outraged at a variety of new taxes levied on the colonies without representation, dumped the tea into the harbor; the king at that time was King George." Students should also record their own observations to the facts they have read. For example, "If I were a colonist, I would do the same thing that they did; it is totally unfair to make a rule for someone to follow without their input; it reminds me of the rule my parents made for my curfew; someone like King George will not stand for this; things will get worse for the colonists." When students return to class the next day, ask them to work in cooperative groups to share both their facts and personal observations with each other. After groups have ample time to discuss their notes and observations, ask each group to select one observation that they found most interesting to share with the class. Discuss how making conscientious observations affected their reading and understanding of the material.

My Idea

Jot down one idea for this metacognitive tool.

_____

_____

_____

_____

_____

_____

_____

_____

_____

_____

_____

_____

_____

_____

My Reflection

What I Did

Log your use of the idea. Explain what you actually did, giving some details but mostly just the "big idea."

_____

_____

_____

_____

_____

_____

_____

_____

_____

_____

_____

_____

_____

What I Think

Reflect on the activity. What are the pluses and minuses? What other thoughts do you have?

_____

_____

_____

_____

_____

_____

_____

_____

_____

_____

_____

_____

_____

Afterthoughts

SECTION
III

EVALUATING
Strategies for Students to Use

It's what you learn after you know it all that counts.

—John Wonder

Metacognitive evaluation strategies are much like the mirror in a powder compact. Both serve to magnify the image; allow for careful scrutiny; and provide an "up-close and personal" view. When one opens the compact and looks in the mirror, only a selected portion of the face is reflected back, but that particular part is magnified so that every nuance, every flaw and every bump is blatantly in view; inspection is made easier with the enlarged picture.

Similarly, when students look back on their learning through various metacognitive evaluation tools, they often select particular parts for reflective assessment. They want to understand the nuances, ponder the flaws and analyze the bumps. Through metacognitive evaluation, students are given the larger view in order to learn, grow and develop from the inspection process.

As Costa says, "what is inspected, is respected." What is open for close analysis and evaluation is of value—otherwise, students wouldn't spend the time needed to properly evaluate their behavior.

It is assumed, of course, that when one checks one's image in a magnifying mirror, one is doing so in order to make the refinements necessary to reflect a pleasing image. So too, in the metacognitive techniques for self-evaluation. As students look over their work, they key in on certain aspects and use the reflected data in refining or revising their work. For the details and subtleties of anything are readily apparent when revealed under the magnified eye of a mirrored image.

EVALUATING

10

STRATEGIES

1. *Thumbs Up/Thumbs Down* [PMI] . . . 191

2. *Choose Your Spot* [The Human Graph] . . . 201

3. *Mrs. Potter's Questions* [Evaluating] . . . 211

4. *A Revolving Door* [The Portfolio Registry] . . . 221

5. *Connecting Elephants* [How Can I Use This?] . . . 231

6. *The Big Idea* [Generalizing] . . . 241

7. *Checkmate!* [Self-Administered Checklists] . . . 251

8. *What? So What? Now What?* [Student-Led Conferences] . . . 261

9. *Storytime!* [Anecdotes] . . . 271

10. *Double-Talk* [Double-Entry Journals] . . . 281

STRATEGY 1

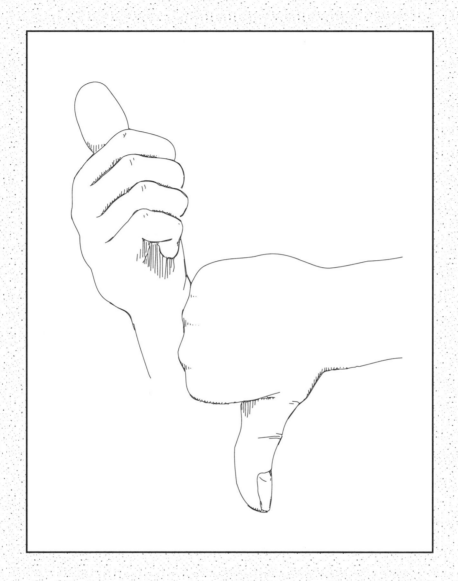

Thumbs Up/ Thumbs Down

[PMI]

PMI

What

Plus. Minus. Interesting.
Plus, minus, interesting.
Plus? Minus? Interesting?
Plus! Minus! Interesting!

Regardless of how one punctuates for emphasis, de Bono's (1983) brilliant PMI strategy dictates discerning comments that help one evaluate all sides of an issue, an idea, or a learning episode. The PMI is one of the most clear, yet comprehensive tools available for evaluation or self-evaluation. It is clear in its focus and comprehensive in its scope. First, one delineates the pluses or positive results of a learning episode; the upside, so to speak. Then, the downside or the minuses are reviewed; drawbacks or barriers are profiled. And finally, serendipitous statements are gathered, not pluses, not minuses, but thoughts of interest; comments, questions, and connections that the learner makes.

In addition, the PMI is comprehensive in its scope because inherent in the strategy is the need to survey all perspectives—the good, the bad, and the ugly! By utilizing the PMI, the learner automatically looks at all the angles and in doing so, evaluates the whole picture.

For example, upon completing her doctoral dissertation and during her oral defense, one graduate student was exposed to the PMI strategy when a professor on the committee asked, "What are the strengths of your study? Where are the downsides of the study, the places where you were stuck? And what is interesting about how you got unstuck?"

Another PMI example involving younger students is illustrated in a primary classroom as the teacher asks students to list the things they thought were pluses about their trip to the zoo, the things they thought were minuses, and things of interest that happened that were neither a plus nor a minus, but just things that impressed them. Their completed class chart looked similar to this:

TRIP TO THE ZOO

P (+)	• the snakes were great • the best part was when the elephant laid down • lunch
M (-)	• the smells were bad • when one group missed the bus
I (?)	• the funny noises of the baboon • teacher broke her sandal and had to walk barefoot

PMI

The PMI evaluates with simplicity and clarity, the positives, the negatives, and the neutrals. It is a viable, quick study of a situation that fosters a complete look because it asks for opposing views or perspectives.

The rationale supporting the PMI strategy is embedded in the extensive work of Edward de Bono (1973). His work on "lateral thinking" is probably the most recognized strategy for thinking about a situation horizontally, or creatively, rather than vertically. De Bono also has produced a number of works on how the mind is able to perceive things from many angles and, thus, generate creative solutions to challenges.

For example, in his book, *Six Thinking Hats* (1985) de Bono codes each hat a different color and the particular color signals a way of thinking about the problem. The red hat guides thinking emotionally, while the black hat triggers critical, evaluative thinking. By symbolically changing hats, the mode of thinking is shifted to a new and different perspective.

Although the "lateral thinking" and "six hats" strategies are targeted to the business world, the concept of reviewing situations through multiple perspectives also permeates de Bono's materials for the educational arena. In fact, the PMI is just one of the sixty strategies presented in the CoRT thinking resources.

While the plus, minus, and interesting categories force shifts in thinking about the pros and cons, the OPV (Other Point of View) also forces a shift toward another perspective.

Of course, the value of analyzing an idea from multiple perspectives enhances research of any sort. For example, in qualitative studies, the concept of triangulation supports the idea of three different perspectives of an observation: participant-observer; observer; and unobtrusive evidence. By gathering three views, a more critical evaluation is possible.

With the PMI the concept of different viewpoints also validates an evaluation. Just as any review is enhanced when critics disagree and present opposing views, the PMI naturally forces a valid critique. Interesting, just as with Siskel and Ebert in their film critiques, when one may

PMI

state a plus (thumbs up) while the other sees the same element as a minus (thumbs down), the PMI may also reveal how one aspect can be both a plus and a minus.

For example, as students process the cooperation during an activity, one may say it was a plus to have four people in the group, because there were more ideas, while another member may cite that as a minus because it was too confusing or too slow with four people. Regardless of the ambiguity, at least both positive and negative responses are sought when one utilizes the PMI strategy.

 Introduction of the PMI is most easily done in what is often called a content-free lesson. In fact, de Bono uses a hypothetical situation in which students ponder the pluses, minuses, and interesting aspects of taking the seats out of buses. Naturally, they have quite an animated debate as they look at not only the drawbacks to having a bus with no seats, but also the benefits of this rather radical idea.

Following this kind of introduction to PMI, students can be given more opportunities to think about the pluses, minuses, and interesting aspects of almost anything. For instance, the whole class can PMI their behavior at the assembly program. What were the positives of their behavior? What were the negatives? And what was just interesting? Of course, from the analysis, a discussion may follow with suggestions for change.

To take the PMI into a more content-focused activity, partners may PMI their topics for their upcoming research papers in social studies, or their strategies for solving a difficult math problem. Individually, students may PMI their reaction to a personal problem.

However, the important thing to remember when one uses the PMI strategy is to allow equal opportunity for responses to all three areas: the plus, the minus, and the interesting. Sometimes, because of time constraints, the pluses, which naturally come first, get more air time than the minuses or interesting aspects.

Another caution is to allow a healthy look at the negatives, even if one instinctively favors the more positive responses. By airing the minuses, as well as the other, a fair evaluation is

PMI

more likely. Remember, in an assessment, one wants to have the whole picture, so nurture the responses in all areas—the "P," the "M," and the "I"—or you will be the selling the strategy short of its real potential.

In fact, once students become familiar with the idea of multiple perspectives through the use of the PMI, it becomes difficult *not* to consider all three aspects!

hen Of all the evaluation strategies, the PMI is probably the one that is more adaptable to any classroom situation. It can be articulated quickly in duos, agreed upon in a think-pair-share strategy, discussed more fully in small groups, or charted with input from the entire class.

Because the PMI is so readily learned and so quickly embraced by both teachers and students alike, it can be used quite informally in many classroom settings. Also, in a bit more formal manner, students might incorporate the PMI as a journal entry or as an analysis technique for shaping a literary critique or lab write-up. The PMI is an all-weather strategy. It works in just about any situation, whether it be in the classroom, in the staff room, or in personal life scenarios. Try it!

LOG ENTRY: SCIENCE TEST

P(+)	The test was balanced with short answers and essay questions.
M(−)	I studied the wrong stuff.
I(?)	I like the idea of submitting questions we had made up.

One Idea

 Elementary school students can practice the PMI strategy in pairs. First, have students write about an invention they would like to create. It can be anything, as long as it has not already been created. Provide the students with some examples of your own. Students are to describe their inventions in one paragraph. Encourage them to give as many details and be as specific as possible so that the reader will be able to clearly imagine the invention. After students write their paragraphs, have them trade papers with a partner and have each student then evaluate his or her partner's creation, using a PMI chart.

Have students list as many pluses, minuses, and interesting aspects of the invention as they can, solely from reading their partner's paragraphs. After that, have students ask their partners questions in order to get more information. Remind students that they must consider all three areas to get a complete picture of the invention. Finally, have students share their PMIs with the original creator of the invention and see if they agree with their partner's PMI evaluation of their invention.

If disagreements arise, encourage students to discuss their differences. Ask students if some aspects can fall under more than one category and why.

To finish the activity, have students draw a picture of their invention. Post the drawings with the PMI charts around the classroom. Allow students to tour all the drawings.

This PMI activity can be adapted for older students as well. Middle and high school students can discuss the ramifications of the inventions. Ask students: Will the invention put anyone out of work? Will the invention offend any ethnic or religious group? Will the resources needed to build the invention always be available?

My Idea

Jot down one idea for this metacognitive tool.

My Reflection

What I Did

Log your use of the idea. Explain what you actually did, giving some details but mostly just the "big idea."

_____

_____

_____

_____

_____

_____

_____

_____

_____

_____

_____

_____

_____

What I Think

Reflect on the activity. What are the pluses and minuses? What other thoughts do you have?

_____

_____

_____

_____

_____

_____

_____

_____

_____

_____

_____

_____

_____

Afterthoughts

_____

_____

_____

_____

_____

_____

_____

_____

_____

_____

_____

_____

_____

_____

_____

_____

_____

STRATEGY 2

Choose Your Spot

[THE HUMAN GRAPH]

THE HUMAN GRAPH

hat Imagine a line or axis across the front of a classroom with students standing at various spots on the line, creating, in essence, a vertical bar graph of humans. By selecting particular positions along the imaginary line, and standing one behind the other when more than one person chooses a spot, the students actually become the graph. Each student is part of the whole picture.

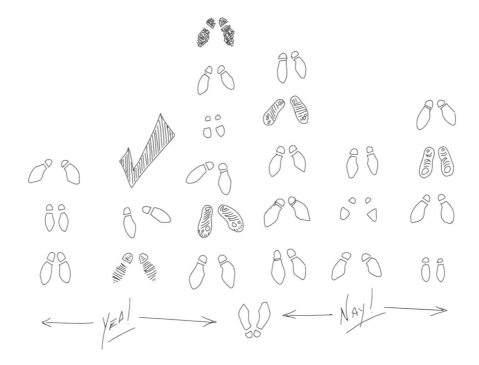

This actual graphing of student reactions is called the human graph because it presents a picture of their ideas just as if they had recorded it on paper. However, the human graph has a distinct advantage over the general bar graph represented on paper. For with the human graph, positions can be readily changed as new information and data are received. So the human graph is a living, moving graph that invites negotiation and compromise as positions are shifted and reflected in the configuration of the final graph.

For example, high school students are given this scenario: The school authorities, in their effort to fight the drug problems on campus, decide to do an unannounced locker check. Decide to what degree you agree or disagree with their action. Be prepared to give reasons.

THE HUMAN GRAPH

Students then select their stance and line up accordingly while the teacher samples reasons. Students not only take a public stand but they also advocate their position. As they hear the various rationales, they can choose to change their opinion simply by moving to a new position on the graph.

This human graph strategy offers a multitude of "teachable moments" for meaningful reflection and metacognitive awareness. For example, as the human graph evolves, students can analyze:

(Decisiveness)	how quickly one reaches a decision
(Intensity)	how far to the side one moves
(Flexibility)	how often one changes his or her mind
(Values)	how one comes to a decision
(Empathy)	how one reacts in a minority/majority position
(Personality)	how one reflects his or her attitudes and choices

The rationale for using the strategy of the human graph to evaluate one's opinions is illustrated in this all-too-common scenario: the newspaper headlines announce that according to a national assessment survey, students across the nation are unable to write a paragraph that advocates a position and supports that position with details.

In order to change that situation, utilizing the human graph at opportune moments gives students practice in making decisions, verbally supporting those decisions, and then, in the follow-up discussion, metacognitively evaluating their decision-making skills.

Just as all cooperative learning strategies provide opportunities for students to articulate their thinking, the human graph is designed to facilitate that articulation. For students are encouraged to not only take a position, but they are expected to justify their position as well.

THE HUMAN GRAPH

While Nancy Johnson's initial use of the human graph called for students to choose one side or the other, Fogarty and Bellanca (1989) expand the graph to delineate degrees of intensity. In Johnson's model a sample question is: Would you rather be a mountain climber or a deep-sea diver? Students select one or the other side and vocalize their reasoning.

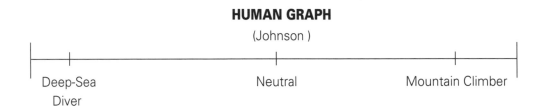

In the Fogarty and Bellanca model, the question is still: Would you rather be a mountain climber or a deep-sea diver? But in this situation, students select varying positions along a spectrum of positions. This refinement in their stands designates degrees of agreement or disagreement.

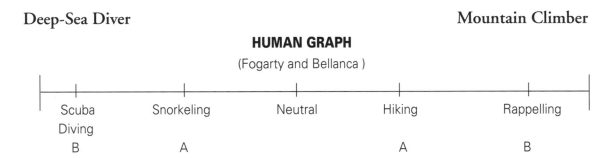

The rationale for the decisions is of utmost importance in both models. It is imperative that students justify their opinion by supporting their reasoning with details.

Also, the research on metacognition is supported fully in the model only when discussion or reflection follows about why and how decisions about the graph are made. This is the metacognitive moment in the human graph strategy, when students become aware of not only what their opinions are, but how and why their ideas develop.

THE HUMAN GRAPH

**How** The human graph is most easily introduced by actually putting masking tape on the floor, with the incremental positions clearly marked. This saves a lot of confusion as students execute that first graph. Also, the first few graphs are easiest for students if the problem is somewhat value free. For example, Gordon's (1961) Synectics model uses forced relationships, in which two unlike things are compared. They seem somewhat whimsical, but are effective for warming up with the human graph. Questions include:

Which is quicker, black or yellow?

What takes up more space, a pickle or a pear?

What are you, a door or a window?

Which is sadder, jello or a slipper?

Which is wiser, a squirrel or an alligator?

Each idea is suggested, students take their position on the taped line, and the teacher samples the students for reasons, rationales, and relevant comments. Then, the teacher asks students to make some generalizations about the activity: "How easy was your decision? How does it feel being the only two on that side? Why did you change sides after that last comment?"

Interestingly, once students grasp the concept of physically graphing themselves to take a reading on particular issues, they begin to spontaneously suggest using the graph to sort out an idea or to settle an argument or debate. For example, one student suggested, "Let's graph it," as the class was trying to decide on how they would report to parents about their progress on parent night. Their graph designations looked like this:

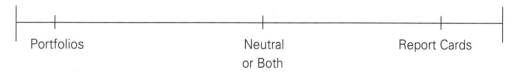

Portfolios   Neutral   Report Cards
or Both

Another group used the human graph to report their opinions on presidential candidates.

Candidate A   No Opinion   Candidate B

THE HUMAN GRAPH

Again, perhaps the most startling results of the human graph lie in the area of self-evaluative, metacognitive awareness. One child initiated this insightful response to the teacher. "You know, Ms. Smith, I'm always in the middle. I can never seem to decide one way or the other. I usually want it both ways." Another student said, "I wait to see where Johnny goes on the graph, then I follow. We're always together; even on the human graph."

Both of their statements are quite revealing and in the articulation of them, a door is opened for the teacher to talk to his or her students about their decision-making processes.

 The human graph is appropriate from the primary classroom to the adult staff room. It works with groups of all sizes, as well. However, when the group is large (thirty plus), sampling a few answers is the only way to expedite the activity. Yet, participants can be directed to process their own decision-making process in a personal journal entry. In this way, the reflection is facilitated, but it stays private. Still, metacognitive thinking has been activated so students are more likely to think again in another parallel situation about how they make decisions.

An opportune time to introduce the human graph into students' repertoire of metacognitive evaluation strategies is early in the semester. Use of the graphing technique signals similar things to students:

- Personal opinions are expected.
- Decision-making skills are valued.
- Justification and thoughtfulness is standard procedure.
- Responsibility is to be taken by the students.
- Issues are often ambiguous and paradoxical.
- Positions can be negotiated.

With this set of issues on the table, students can only benefit from early use of the strategy and frequent opportunities to revisit the human graph.

One Idea

The human graph activity can be an interesting change in routine for middle and high school students. They welcome the opportunity to get out of their seats for a while to learn.

Begin the activity by showing the students a newspaper headline. Ask students to predict what the article will be about. Write the students' guesses on the board.

Next, have students read the entire article. They may read to themselves silently or in small cooperative groups. Then, have the students decide on the major issue or debate that the article presents. Have students form the issue as a statement such as: "The President should send military troops to aid a troubled nation" or "It is a good idea to remove the troops from the troubled nation." Ask students if they agree or disagree with the statement.

Tell the students that they are now going to form a human graph to demonstrate how everyone feels. With masking tape, construct a horizontal line on the floor and mark these degrees of agreement along the line: Strongly Disagree, Mildly Disagree, Neutral, Mildly Agree, and Strongly Agree.

Have the students get out of their seats and move to a position on the graph. Tell students that when they select a position, they must be prepared to justify their reasons. Call on some students and elicit their reasons for choosing their position. Let students know that it is O.K. to change their opinion and move to a different spot on the floor. Ask the students what they see happening. Are there many students in one place and none in another?

Finally, have students reflect on the activity in their journals. Have them write a journal entry in which they explain (1) the position they took and why, (2) what happened when it was time to pick a position, and (3) why some students switched positions as others explained their reasons?

My Idea

Jot down one idea for this metacognitive tool.

_____

_____

_____

_____

_____

_____

_____

_____

_____

_____

_____

_____

_____

_____

_____

_____

My Reflection

What I Did

Log your use of the idea. Explain what you actually did, giving some details but mostly just the "big idea."

_____

_____

_____

_____

_____

_____

_____

_____

_____

_____

_____

_____

_____

What I Think

Reflect on the activity. What are the pluses and minuses? What other thoughts do you have?

_____

_____

_____

_____

_____

_____

_____

_____

_____

_____

_____

_____

_____

Afterthoughts

STRATEGY 3

Mrs. Potter's Questions

[EVALUATING]

EVALUATING

What Reflective questions that cause students to think back over their just-completed work often are composed of the following:

1. What was your purpose?
2. What are the strengths?
3. What are the weaknesses?
4. What else is needed?

To make these questions more readily remembered, Mrs. Potter (a fictitious character) is introduced to the students. In the strategy called Mrs. Potter's Questions, the questions follow that same genre, but they are worded a bit more conversationally. Mrs. Potter, a seasoned teacher, asks her students to evaluate their work by reviewing and responding to these four questions. She simply asks:

1. What were you trying to do?
2. What went well?
3. What would you do differently next time?
4. Do you need any help?

As students address each of the four questions, they actually critique their own work and participate in the self-evaluative process. For example, a high school student may review Mrs. Potter's Questions following a lab experiment and make a journal entry:

Bio Lab Experiment: The Microscope

What was I trying to do?	View and draw the 5 slides for later recognition and analysis.
What went well?	My diagrams were clear and accurate.
What would I do differently?	I would read the book first so I'd know what to look for.
Do I need any help?	It took me forever to focus the microscope on the various slides.

EVALUATING

Similarly, for younger students, Mrs. Potter's Questions might be done in a whole class review following a unit study of plants. In this situation, students respond to Mrs. Potter's Questions and the teacher records samples of their responses on a large chart. This review is easily done following a learning experiment and guides students toward self-regulatory activity as they look back and process their work.

While the strategy of Mrs. Potter's Questions seems almost too obvious as a means of metacognitively evaluating one's work, it is just this simplicity that sometimes creates the problem. It is so easy that teachers often overlook its inherent value and tend to leave it out. As the lesson winds down and time is short, these four simple questions are skipped over and the deep metacognitive reflection is missed. The teacher might ask, "How'd you do?" but this question, unlike Mrs. Potter's, tends to foster more cognitive answers: "I got two wrong," or "I did great." Mrs. Potter's Questions require more self-analysis and cause reflective comments as students recall not just what they did, but how it went. It is looking back and at the same time looking into one's self.

Based on Bloom's *Taxonomy of Educational Objectives* (1956), six levels of thinking and questioning are distinguished: knowledge, comprehension, application, analysis, synthesis, and evaluation. While Mrs. Potter's Questions span all six levels, the focus is emphatically on the highest—evaluation. As a matter of fact, the purpose of Mrs. Potter's four questions is to cause reflection, to look back and assess the learning. Students primed in self-evaluative techniques find Mrs. Potter's Questions easy to remember and therefore readily available to use in any number of situations. The four questions become quite automatic. What was I trying to do? What did I do well? What will I change? Do I need any help?

Interestingly, the story of Mrs. Potter's Questions is a story of simple replication. A young man, about to student teach at a high school in southern Illinois, was assigned to Mimi Potter's English literature class. During the course of his work with what was then referred to

EVALUATING

as his "critic teacher," this young apprentice noticed that after every lesson he taught, Mrs. Potter would sit him down and ask him the same four questions: "What was your purpose? What went well? What would you do differently? Do you need any help from me?" And, he also noticed that as he struggled to answer the four queries, he not only "relived the highs of the experience, but he was able to readily see alternatives and enhancements that could easily be incorporated if he were to teach a similar lesson.

This young teacher, impressed with the power of Mrs. Potter's Questions, inadvertently found himself using the very same evaluation techniques with his own students years later. After working on an assignment, he would ask: What were you trying to do? What went well? What would you do differently? Do you need any help? Thus, the legacy of Mrs. Potter's Questions was born and lives on today, but with a deeper appreciation of their magical, reflective powers. Since the concept of metacognition is now recognized and valued as a potent tool for reflective transfer, Mrs. Potter's Questions take on added value as a tool to promote the transfer of learning (Fogarty, Perkins & Barell, 1992).

***

 Introducing Mrs. Potter's Questions to the children, in one elementary school, the teachers created a huge hall bulletin board display featuring Mrs. Potter and her four (now famous) questions.

1. What were you expected to do?

2. In this assignment, what did you do well?

3. If you had to do this task over, what would you do differently?

4. What help do you need from me?

Throughout the year, as the seasons change, Mrs. Potter's attire changes. When it snows outside, it also snows in the display and Mrs. Potter dons her overcoat. When it is sunny and

EVALUATING

warm, the sun appears in the display and Mrs. Potter wears only her dress and a large apron. But, regardless of the weather conditions, and the changing of garments, Mrs. Potter's Questions remain the same. And, naturally, over time, the children can rattle off these questions in the blink of an eye.

With older students, the four questions can be introduced as small group discussion questions following a project or for individual reflection in a journal or learning log. However, more pervasive measures have been used to introduce these questions to high schoolers.

One teacher in Grosse Pointe, Michigan, not only formally presents Mrs. Potter and her four famous questions, but also introduces "Uncle Ben" Bloom's (1956) Taxonomy to his students. So, as students in his class work on their assignments, they are able to analyze Uncle Ben's six levels of thinking that they are using or that are evidenced in their readings. And, following the task, they are then able to reflect on the learning using Mrs. Potter's four questions. The two techniques are so naturally embraced by the students, one day a young girl asked, "Is Mrs. Potter related to Uncle Ben?"

Whether or not you decide to introduce Mrs. Potter's Questions with such flourish, the simplicity of the questions and the richness of their results warrants some initiation of the idea with your students.

It seems most likely that Mrs. Potter's Questions will be used toward the close of an activity or as a culminating activity. This is when evaluative reflections foster the deepest contemplation. This is also when students probably have the opportunity to think about meaningful transfer and application beyond the lesson. In fact, it is during this evaluation process that the mindful abstraction necessary for remote or far-reaching transfer is probable (Fogarty, Perkins & Barell, 1992). It is in the evaluation and reflection phase when learners are more likely to extrapolate the essence of an idea and think about other potential uses. This evaluation stage becomes the golden opportunity to lead students toward relevant transfer.

EVALUATING

But to foster that transfer, certain questions seem more conducive to reflective bridging; Mrs. Potter's Questions fit that criterion. The four questions dictate responses that judge, weigh, and critique for future use.

Think back for a moment about what you just read:

> What was your purpose?
> What did you do well?
> What would you change?
> Do you need further help?

You see, Mrs. Potter's Questions guide a momentary reflection that forces meaning to the reading experience just completed. Mrs. Potter's Questions help you evaluate and think reflectively for long-term learning.

In yet another vein, the idea of previewing Mrs. Potter's Questions prior to the learning episode is, perhaps, an enhancement to the strategy. By signaling students before the lesson to the four reflective questions, they may be better prepared to answer them later. This quick preview of what is to come may guide students to self-evaluate along the way.

Remember, too, that the list of four questions can be shortened to two or tailored to the situation as needed. In brief, the question of "when" to use Mrs. Potter's Questions is best answered with the reverse question, "When wouldn't you use them?" They are universally appropriate.

One Idea

 Help students become accustomed to using Mrs. Potter's questions by asking them to select a recent project, paper, or homework assignment for evaluation. Explain that they may collaborate with a partner to help critique each other's work. Students can take turns role playing the part of Mrs. Potter asking the four questions: What were you trying to do? What went well? What would you do differently next time? Do you need any help?

Tell the class that it is important for the partner asking the questions to give the other student ample time to think. They should reflect on their work themselves before any discussion with their partner. Partners may help students with ideas and prompts, but the main goal is to have students learn how to reflect on their own work. However, since the fourth question is most appropriate for partners to give advice, the partner playing the role of Mrs. Potter can offer his or her help and support freely. Students can jot down their thoughts and comments as notes during the entire process.

Make sure students realize that this process can be exercised on their own with any assignment in any subject area. All they need to do is ask themselves Mrs. Potter's four questions.

My Idea

Jot down one idea for this metacognitive tool.

_____

_____

_____

_____

_____

_____

_____

_____

_____

_____

_____

_____

_____

_____

_____

My Reflection

What I Did

Log your use of the idea. Explain what you actually did, giving some details but mostly just the "big idea."

_____

_____

_____

_____

_____

_____

_____

_____

_____

_____

_____

_____

_____

What I Think

Reflect on the activity. What are the pluses and minuses? What other thoughts do you have?

_____

_____

_____

_____

_____

_____

_____

_____

_____

_____

_____

_____

_____

Afterthoughts

_____

_____

_____

_____

_____

_____

_____

_____

_____

_____

_____

_____

_____

_____

_____

_____

STRATEGY 4

A Revolving Door

[THE PORTFOLIO REGISTRY]

THE PORTFOLIO REGISTRY

 The use of portfolios for evaluating one's work, a common practice with artists, designers, and architects, is now gaining popularity as a tool in the authentic assessment movement in schools. For years, the writing folder has been promoted as a way to assess the development of student writing over time. Similarly, the portfolio is seen as a way to gather a number of student samples as representative of their work. The portfolio, according to Ferrara & McTighe (1992), resembles a photo album of the student's efforts versus the traditional, single snapshot afforded through the graded report card.

However, the portfolio registry, Dietz (1993), refines the portfolio process and, in fact, actually moves the portfolio development into the realm of self-regulatory evaluation. There are two distinct steps in portfolio development: collecting and selecting (Burke, 1993). According to the experts, gathering an assortment of artifacts to represent student progress is the collecting stage. Then, in order to shape the collection into a manageable piece, the selection process comes next. This is where the portfolio registry makes an entrance. The registry becomes the record of the selections. As students collect artifacts for their portfolios, they must then reflect on their final selections, including some while rejecting others. Based on this process, they keep scrupulous records in their portfolio registry about their selections and their reasons for those selections, about their withdrawals and the reasons for the withdrawals.

The portfolio registry is just that, a registry of what artifacts are contained in the portfolio. The registry includes dates that items are placed in the portfolio with comments about why they were selected, but it also presents information on items that are taken out of the portfolio, with dates and rationale for those decisions, too.

For example, a sixth grade portfolio registry might include entries similar to these:

PORTFOLIO REGISTRY

DATE	IN	ITEM	OUT	COMMENT
9-25-93	X	Autobiography		1st draft
10-8-93		Invention Report	X	Invention already seen by parents and teacher
11-20-93		Sheet Music	X	Accomplishment
12-1-93	X	Brochure on 10K		Goal
1-14-94	X	Math test		1st one I finished all questions.

Name: _Timothy Scott_   _Grade 6_

THE PORTFOLIO REGISTRY

Although the registry does not take the place of a personal oral review of the artifacts in the portfolio, with a running commentary of the whats, whys, and hows, the portfolio registry does serve as a guided tour. The registry also provides a bird's-eye view of the whole portfolio; at a glance, one knows the kind of items that are inside and some insight into why they are selected. The registry lists items, dates of entry and withdrawal, and comments of insight and self-awareness.

———————————◆———————————

hy The rationale for the portfolio registry as a metacognitive evaluation tool is obvious. It fosters self-understanding about why decisions are made as well as what the decisions actually are. Metacognition calls for awareness and control over one's thinking and behavior and the registry offers both. The collection process provides awareness of the students' learnings in the selection/rejection process.

The registry provides a record and forces reflection by its very nature, for it is impossible to keep everything. Once students begin the selection and rejection of items, they must analyze, evaluate, and rank the items. In the prioritization process, values surface and insights into oneself begin to emerge.

According to Dietz (1993), the portfolio registry, used with adult learners, provides opportunity to self-select and present artifacts that are most representative of what one values. Furthermore, and perhaps as important, the registry sets expectations for not only collecting but also for selecting. The registry signals the abundance or overabundance of items. Just as with the portfolio presentation of an artist's choices, selected tidbits whet the appetite while a whole meal becomes burdensome and sometimes indigestible. A manageable portfolio with carefully selected and personally documented item entries is far more telling than a lengthy, unedited version of personal ramblings.

Burke (1993) also suggests the importance of the selection process must not be slighted when using portfolios effectively. It seems that the registry is the additional element in the portfolio model that promotes "selective abandonment" and "judicious inclusion" of items

THE PORTFOLIO REGISTRY

that Art Costa refers to in setting curricular priorities. However, it must be noted that the registry is not merely a table of contents or an index. It is far more than either of those traditional listings. The portfolio registry is more like an anecdotal record of the entries over time.

———◆———

How

As students begin collecting artifacts of their work for their portfolios, an introductory lesson is in order. In this instructional episode, the teacher introduces the idea of organizing the items for easy management. For older students, a sample registry is presented with an explanation of how to use it: Date each entry, mark appropriately if the item is being included or excluded, comment on why it is going in or coming out.

However, for younger students, a formal registry may seem too complicated. In this case, a more informal registry may be utilized. Instead of having students keep an ongoing record of every entry, younger students may simply practice the written entry as a verbal entry. In other words, students pair up, once a week, and take turns telling each other one thing they are putting in their portfolio and one thing they are taking out. This oral practice sets the stage for later, more formalized entries that become written records. In both cases, the oral and the written, students become reflective and self-evaluative.

Yet, once young students experience the process of "collecting, selecting, and reflecting" through the portfolio registry, the registry itself takes on as much importance as the artifact portfolio. For it is in this reflective stage that the portfolio takes on meaning. It is much easier to appreciate an artifact when the artist sets the context for the artifact. So, too, is it true for the student portfolio. It is much easier to appreciate student development when the chosen artifacts are placed in a meaningful context. For example, the picture is more complete when a student shows a doodle on notebook paper and explains that the doodle page was included because it represents a breakthrough in an idea that had been confusing; in doodling, the idea became concrete. To simply include the doodle with no registry entry comment minimalizes the entry. So, in working with students, emphasis is on both the entry and the registry justification comment.

THE PORTFOLIO REGISTRY

 As with any metacognitive tool, the teachable moment comes at various times. But, it seems prudent to say that whenever portfolios are introduced, the registry idea is also introduced. It is simply an aid to managing the materials and gaining insight into the kinds of things that seem most appropriate. It fosters thoughtful use of the portfolio because students realize that they must not only collect a number of things that show how they have grown and developed, but they must select the items they want and reflect on the justification for these items.

Also, in alluding to the appropriate time to introduce portfolios and portfolio registries, it follows that the question of frequency comes up. How often do students make entries in their portfolios and how often do they record their entries? First, every artifact warrants an entry. So if students review their portfolios once a month, they complete the registry once a month, so it is always up-to-date.

Now, in terms of frequency, portfolio management once a month may be enough at the upper levels because of time constraints, but once a week might be a more appropriate time frame for the younger students as they review their work, collect some possible items, and select the ones they want to put in. Then, they justify their choices. The entries can simply be discussed or noted earlier or young students can make a written entry, also. However, their registry may be a more preferable registry, with each entry made on a separate card (3 x 5) that is then attached to the item. This registry model resembles a tag and is placed on the artifact.

Item:	*Puppet Picture*
Date:	*11-16-93*
Comment:	*Wanted to keep the puppet at home.*
	Picture shows how I made it.
Name:	*Brian Mitchell*

Once students begin the process, they continue using the portfolio registry whenever they handle their portfolio. It is really quite easy.

One Idea

 Give younger students extra practice in the thought processes behind the creation of a portfolio registry by having them collect one week's worth of their work for evaluation. After modeling and practicing the process in class several times, both with the teacher and peers, have students practice the process with their parents. First, choose a Friday afternoon to give students class time to review their assignments from the week. Tell them to *choose* four items that they would like to include in their portfolios. On a Post-it note, have students *record why* they chose that item and the date.

Now, tell them to take the four items home in a folder and during the course of the weekend, discuss them with a parent, making sure that they explain the reasoning behind their selections. (Sending a letter home to parents ahead of time to make them aware of the special homework assignment is a good idea.) When students return to class on Monday, allow them to share the results of their weekend discussions with their parents. Explain that this week they will again save their work for evaluation. However, this time they must choose *two items to add* to their folders and *two items to remove*. Again, ask that students discuss their selections and omissions with their parents.

Older students may prefer to work in cooperative groups to discuss and share their written portfolio registries, rather than discussing them with parents.

My Idea

Jot down one idea for this metacognitive tool.

_____

_____

_____

_____

_____

_____

_____

_____

_____

_____

_____

_____

_____

_____

_____

My Reflection

What I Did

Log your use of the idea. Explain what you actually did, giving some details but mostly just the "big idea."

_____

_____

_____

_____

_____

_____

_____

_____

_____

_____

_____

_____

_____

_____

What I Think

Reflect on the activity. What are the pluses and minuses? What other thoughts do you have?

_____

_____

_____

_____

_____

_____

_____

_____

_____

_____

_____

_____

_____

_____

Afterthoughts

STRATEGY 5

Connecting Elephants

[HOW CAN I USE THIS?]

HOW CAN I USE THIS?

at Connecting elephants is a strategy that aids student self-evaluation and transfer of learning. It involves three imaginary elephants marching into a circus tent with each elephant holding in its trunk the tail of another elephant. The three elephants are connected in an unending circle as they parade around the center ring. These three elephants represent three BIG questions: What's the big idea? How does this connect to other big ideas? How can I use this big idea? The following illustrations suggest the connections.

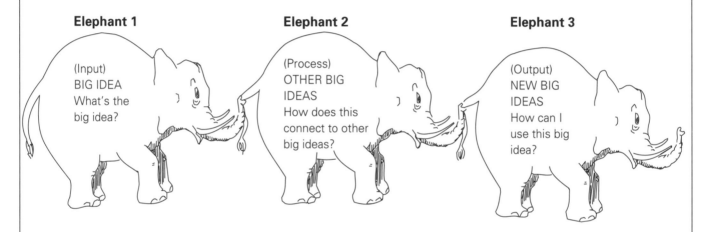

By asking, "What's the big idea?", students focus on the input of the learning or activity, evaluate their understandings, and synthesize the information into a big idea. Students actually extrapolate these big ideas and make valid generalizations that can be more easily connected to other ideas.

This is where the elephant connects to the next one. That is to say, the student takes the big idea from the new learning, and deliberately tries to connect it to past experiences or prior knowledge. By making explicit connections from an emergent idea to a previously held idea, the student forces further synthesis as the ideas are processed in an integrated way. Hence, there are now two elephants connected in our imaginary scenario.

Finally, a third elephant is joined to the first two as the students think about how the new idea, connected to former ideas, can be used in new ways. They are always asking themselves, "What's the big idea here? How does it connect with what I know?" And, "How can I use this idea?" The thoughtful process of connecting elephants gently pushes the idea of

HOW CAN I USE THIS?

metacognitive transfer. Each connected elephant represents a stage in the evaluation process, but by connecting incrementally, students are not only more thorough, but also more self-regulating in their application. They are making applications that are personally relevant.

For example, as a student learns about statistics she extrapolates a big idea: statistics requires scrupulous data collection to yield reliable and valid results. The student tries to connect this idea to one she already knows; data recorded consistently and accurately over time is more likely to give a truer picture than haphazard and/or missed entries. Now, the student thinks about how to use the new idea in a relevant application. Her mind lights on the upcoming marathon that she wants to run. Suddenly, she has an idea. She can use a log to keep track of her running for the next two months. Then, based on that data, how far and how fast she is able to run, she will derive a program for training during the next three months that will result in a successful marathon for her.

Sidney Parnes (1975) says, "If only we could get kids to ask, after a learning, 'What's the big idea, here? How does this connect to what I already know and how can I use this?', we could take learning in this century to new levels." Upon reading that idea, years ago, the concept of facilitating connection making for students became paramount.

In fact, Fogarty, Perkins, and Barell (1992) address the topic of generalizing big ideas in their discussion of how to help with transfer of learning. Generalizations (or big ideas) are not always explicit to students, so some probing or mediation seems to facilitate the development of those generalizations. Coupled with the strategy of making generalizations, Fogarty (1991) pushes the idea of making connections in order to move toward more holistic, integrated models of learning. The two strategies become somewhat synergistic in the connecting elephants technique because students are not only required to search for big ideas and to process those ideas, but they are also asked to connect the emerging ideas and then apply the re-

HOW CAN I USE THIS?

sulting connections to novel situations. This deliberate cognitive connection making is exactly what Perkins & Salomon (1988) refer to as mindful abstraction or bridging for transfer.

———————◆———————

How

Connecting elephants, because of the colorful metaphor, are probably most easily introduced through some sort of graphic. Some primitive drawings on the blackboard or in an overhead transparency will suffice. A more elaborate approach would be to actually create a bulletin board of cut-out or painted elephants—all connected. Of course, the graphics need to be accompanied with a demonstration and/or explanation. But students seem to understand the strategy of connecting elephants quite easily.

Another introductory model that is useful at the upper levels, but really works at any level, is role play. As a processing technique, after a learning, ask students to group in threes. Then, number them one, two, and three and instruct them to role play the idea of connecting elephants. Student one makes a "big idea" statement concerning the lesson just completed; student two makes a connection to an already known big idea; and student three must connect the emergent big idea to a new situation in which it can be used effectively. The connecting elephant trio, in turn, processes big ideas for meaningful transfer.

For example, student one comments on the Boston Tea Party scenario in the social studies text on the Revolutionary War: "One big idea is that sometimes when you're in conflict with another party, you can become violent (throw the tea overboard) or you can react in a calmer manner (boycott the tea)."

Student two takes the big idea and connects it to a big idea he or she already knows: "We learned that conflict can be resolved in many different ways in our cooperative learning groups. One way is to talk about the options."

Student three now connects the big ideas to a relevant situation by applying the ideas to his or her classroom. "I think I've got it. Instead of boycotting the hot lunch program because

HOW CAN I USE THIS?

we believe the meals do not reflect the low-fat contents recommended by nutrition experts, let's gather data that support our efforts and see if we can present it to the administration."

Notice how the scenario of connecting new ideas to old ideas leads to even better ideas. Connecting elephants is a metacognitive reflection tool that leads to evaluation and application.

The best time to introduce connecting elephants as a metacognitive tool is at the close of a unit or lesson in which the big ideas are quite obvious. Social studies or science curricula offer opportunities to extrapolate big ideas easily, but literature is also rich with themes and contextual undercurrents that just jump out with big ideas.

Connecting elephants is appropriate at all levels. As Parnes (1975) eludes to, the more often we can lead students to relevant connection making, the more likely we are to help them internalize the learnings for long term. These deliberate and sometimes tedious attempts to generalize, find the big idea, extrapolate the meaning, connect to prior knowledge, and apply to novel situations require thoughtfulness that often does not occur naturally. Skillful instructors teach these strategies explicitly and mediate the exercises for students until they are able to handle them on their own.

In fact, the scaffolding or mediation is almost a given if this strategy is to become a viable, self-initiated tool for students. They are not always familiar with "reflective thinking and metacognitive connection making" as a reflective, mindful activity. However, with some direct instruction, role plays, and relevant practice, students can continue to "connect elephants" in the classroom and in situations in their lives outside the educational arena.

One Idea

Use the connecting elephants strategy with literature by having students work together in cooperative groups. Use a novel or story that they are currently reading or have read as a class for the basis of the discussions. Ask students to discuss their reading selection and to brainstorm a list of themes they found present in the story. Tell them to *select* one of these themes as the Big Idea. Next, they can discuss how the idea *connects* to something else they know about. Lastly, they should discuss how they can *use* this Big Idea personally. Have them record their connections and then share them with the entire class.

For example, elementary students reading *Miss Rumphius*, by Barbara Cooney, could identify the Big Idea as: A person really can make a difference in the world and make it a better place, like Miss Rumphius did by planting flowers everywhere she went. The connecting idea could include: We've learned from our parents and teachers that we can take care of the earth by not littering and by trying to recycle. The Big Idea can then be applied by the students in a variety of ways, such as: We could do our part to beautify the earth by starting a recycling program at school and picking up trash around the building.

Make sure the cooperative groups share their discussions with the entire class. It is interesting for students to see how other groups made connections and applications with their ideas. Adapt this activity for older students reading novels so that they work individually or in pairs. Do not forget to have students share their work with the rest of the class.

My Idea

Jot down one idea for this metacognitive tool.

_____

_____

_____

_____

_____

_____

_____

_____

_____

_____

_____

_____

_____

_____

_____

_____

My Reflection

What I Did

Log your use of the idea. Explain what you actually did, giving some details but mostly just the "big idea."

_____

_____

_____

_____

_____

_____

_____

_____

_____

_____

_____

_____

What I Think

Reflect on the activity. What are the pluses and minuses? What other thoughts do you have?

_____

_____

_____

_____

_____

_____

_____

_____

_____

_____

_____

_____

Afterthoughts

_____

_____

_____

_____

_____

_____

_____

_____

_____

_____

_____

_____

_____

_____

_____

_____

_____

_____

STRATEGY 6

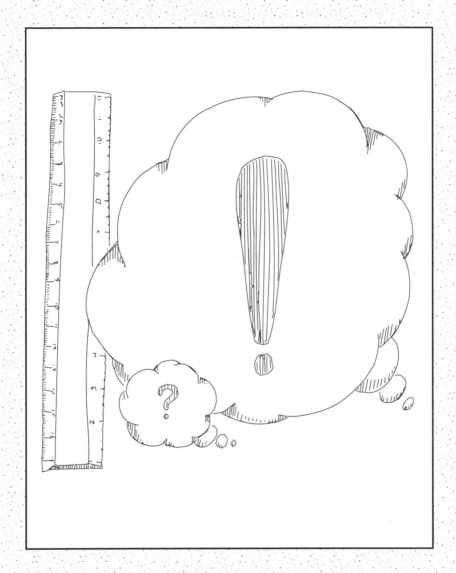

The Big Idea

[GENERALIZING]

GENERALIZING

hat The big idea is not the same as the main idea. The big idea is a generalization that is made based on facts, inferences, and conclusions. The big idea is extrapolated from an activity or learning experience. It is a major learning or idea that seems obvious as a result of the information at hand. The big idea is more often conceptual in nature than topical. It is an idea that undergirds other learnings and branches out into many related areas.

For example, a big idea that occurred following a study of Native Americans is the concept of segregation. While the reservations provide some retribution for lands taken away from Native Americans, the reservation system inherently creates a governmentally imposed separation from other cultural segments of society. This big idea or concept of segregation has applications in many segments of society: economic segregation, racial segregation, and cultural segregation.

By focusing on the big idea of segregation, students are able to readily make connections to various curriculum content. It takes learning from the rote memorization of facts to meaningful exploration of big ideas that impact students' lives in a multitude of ways.

The "big idea of the big idea" is to search for the universal learnings that are embedded in traditional academic content; to move from a curriculum approach that dictates recalling information and facts, to a curricular concern for conceptual learning that relates to many things.

hy Concept attainment or concept development is embedded in the learning theories from Piaget (1972) to Taba (1966) and Bruner (1966). In fact, constructivists believe that knowledge is constructed within the mind of the learner, manipulated according to the personal schemata of each person, and assimilated into that particular context.

GENERALIZING

The rationale for encouraging students to group the big idea lies at the heart of the concept attainment models. In order to make sense of the never-ending stream of incoming information, learners must have a way to organize information into meaningful chunks. These meaningful chunks can be concepts or big ideas that are more manageable in the cognitive realms. Once students become adept at discerning the big ideas in the learnings from the classroom, the more readily they can accommodate and assimilate them into prior contexts and apply them to broader, novel contexts.

To make meaning of the world is what learning is all about. Big ideas facilitate meaning-making by providing broad brush strokes to the emergent pictures. Whatever teachers can do to foster conceptual learning helps students grasp initial ideas and begin the process of constructing their own knowledge. Without promoting "big idea learnings," students are forever burdened with the mundane tasks of recalling facts, data, and trivial informational pieces. With big ideas, the critical connections are made inside the mind of the learner and learning becomes more holistic, more integrated, and easier to anchor for long-term use.

How

"Big ideas" are not easily taught to students of any age. Even teachers have difficulty discerning the conceptual learnings from the topics and factual information. The reason for this is that curriculum content is often organized in textbooks and guides by topics or chapter ideas. Typically, an American history text identifies units of study such as: Explorers, Native Americans, The French and Indian War, The Revolutionary War, The Civil War, and The Industrial Revolution. Yet, if teachers ferret out the big idea, the units look more like this: Exploration, Conflict, Inventions, Human Rights, and Cultural Diversity.

Knowing that the resource materials are organized topically rather than conceptually, the one way to begin teaching for big ideas is to sift out the concepts embedded in the topics.

GENERALIZING

Often, of course, these are found embedded in the teacher guides and instructor resources that are provided with the materials. However, teachers and publishers are beginning to develop thematic models of teaching and learning using the materials as resources.

For example, one teacher settles on the theme of friendship and selects five different novels that deal with the concept of friendship, but, of course, each theme is developed uniquely. Another example is a publisher that organizes a series of stories or excerpts around the theme of perseverance. In both cases, the big ideas of "*friendship*" and "*perseverance*" dominate the learning, with the materials merely vehicles to carry the big ideas along. Now, that is not to say that the details and skills taught in novels and story units are less important. It is just a way to pull out big ideas that are easier for students to connect to in a multitude of situations.

Big ideas, however, do not have to be modeled in full-blown thematic units in the classroom. Although it may be an easy way to start, big idea teaching is a viable, evaluative tool that helps students look over their learnings and metacognitively reflect on the generalizations inherent in the unit of study. Teachers facilitate this by modeling through thematic teaching, but also by giving time and attention to processing and evaluating the learning that takes place in their classrooms.

Teachers can facilitate reflective thinking about the big idea in whole-class, small-group, or individual work. In whole-class discussions, the teacher leads the group toward conceptualization of the big idea through a series of statements or questions that provoke student thinking beyond summarizations of the facts. Statements such as: What is the big idea here? What does this remind you of? and Think of an analogy to prod students beyond the facts about the water cycle they are studying in the science unit to broader, more encompassing ideas about *cycles* or *change*.

Small-group processing for big ideas may be promoted through brainstorming a list of "candidate big ideas" and reaching agreement on one or two. As students study William Faulkner, Toni Morrison, Ernest Hemingway, and Gertrude Stein, they may look for big ideas common to the works of all four novelists. In the younger grades, students may talk with partners or in small groups about the big ideas they have learned in working with magnets. They can then select one big idea to draw and place in their portfolio.

Individually, big ideas are often discovered as students try to write about their learnings in a journal entry or homework assignment. Insights occur that do not seem to happen as frequently when the process of written reflection is missing. There is something about the

GENERALIZING

thoughtfulness and deliberateness necessary when one focuses to write that causes thinking to transcend the mundane and grasp the essence of a work.

Regardless of the method, large or small groups, or individually, big idea generalizations occur most often when shepherded. They need to be paid attention to, if anything of substance is to be extrapolated.

Fostering conceptual learning through the strategy of the big idea seems appropriate for all age groups. Ideally, this kind of summative evaluation of what is important and what generalizations seem pertinent occurs toward the end of a lesson or even after the unit is completed. Students are directed to look back on the experience and try to sort out the overriding ideas on themes from the facts and details. What big learning can they take away from the facts and details? What big learning can they take away from the lesson? What big ideas jump out? How are these big ideas connected to other things they know?

Interestingly, this strategy of finding the big idea or making generalizations seems to be critical to meaningful transfer of learning. While it seems difficult to get students thinking in big ideas initially, once they learn to focus on the major concepts embedded in subject matter content, students seem to continue to self-initiate this strategy as they reflect on their work.

Big ideas can be used with very young students. Simply ask them to turn to a partner and tell the big idea from the science period. Or have them review a big idea they learned that day to report to parents at home. Of course, older students can use journal entries, partnerships, or small group discussions following a lesson, to dig out those "big ideas."

One Idea

 Help elementary students understand the concept of the big idea by creating a "big book of big ideas." A big book is an oversized book, ideal for elementary students because of its big type and illustrations. This can be an ongoing project that the entire class contributes to during the course of several weeks. Over time, students will begin to understand the concept better and internalize it. Model how to make *generalizations* from facts in several lessons in varying content areas. For example, during a math lesson teaching students how to find the area of a rectangle, students may begin to realize after several examples that there is a general rule—length multiplied by width equals the area. When this is discovered, record this on the chalkboard and explain that it is a perfect example of a big idea!

Perhaps during another lesson in health, students discover another generalization—all people, plants, and animals need nutrients, water, and sun. This can also be recorded on the board. Later, during free time, the students can take turns recording and illustrating the big ideas they learned in their big book. After a few weeks, review the progress of the class big book. Discuss the various big ideas they are discovering. Is it becoming easier for them to make generalizations?

With older students you may want to use a "graffiti type" butcher paper display. Students are then invited to write "big ideas" about science or math, etc., on the board as a way to reflect and share their feelings.

My Idea

Jot down one idea for this metacognitive tool.

_____

_____

_____

_____

_____

_____

_____

_____

_____

_____

_____

_____

_____

_____

_____

_____

My Reflection

What I Did

Log your use of the idea. Explain what you actually did, giving some details but mostly just the "big idea."

_____

_____

_____

_____

_____

_____

_____

_____

_____

_____

_____

_____

_____

What I Think

Reflect on the activity. What are the pluses and minuses? What other thoughts do you have?

_____

_____

_____

_____

_____

_____

_____

_____

_____

_____

_____

_____

_____

Afterthoughts

STRATEGY 7

Checkmate!

[SELF-ADMINISTERED CHECKLISTS]

SELF-ADMINISTERED CHECKLISTS

at Checklists, of course, are simply listings of ideas or procedures that cue the learner to check for certain things. Checklists are long memos generated prior to doing a task that capture all the relevant pieces so they can later be reviewed for completion and subsequently checked off as a means of self-evaluating.

Although the checklist seems much too directive to be considered a high-level metacognitive strategy, it does guide one efficiently through an evaluative review. In the course of using the checklist, the students automatically begin to reflect back on what they have just completed. The checklist creates a ready tool for scanning the finished lesson or project as students look for flaws or assets.

For example, a clear, short checklist for completing a bibliography forces students to be accountable for all the needed information.

BIBLIOGRAPHY CHECKLIST

1. Author's name(s)

2. Title(s) [subtitle(s)]

3. Date(s)

4. Publisher

5. City, state

6. Volume, issue number

7. Page numbers

8. Total number of references

9. Types of references

10. Span of years

In addition, the checklist provides a way to look at the big picture. In the illustration above, the checklist includes items about the total number of references, the types of references, plus a cue to review the span of years represented in the bibliography. These items signal the learner to the metacognitive components of evaluation: the how and why of the final product.

SELF-ADMINISTERED CHECKLISTS

Another type of checklist reminds learners to evaluate their own thinking and behavior. For example, as students learn to work in cooperative groups, they evaluate target behaviors or ways of thinking following the group work.

SELF-EVALUATION CHECKLIST

	Y	N
1. I contribute to the group.		
2. I ask questions of others.		
3. I invite questions from others.		
4. I accept others' ideas.		
5. I reach agreements.		

Statements such as the ones listed in the Self-Evaluation Checklist invite learners to reflect on key cooperative behaviors. This reflection leads to a self-assessment that gives learners both awareness and subsequently, control, over their own actions.

———————◆———————

 While Beyer (1987) makes the argument with others that for students to learn to think well, they must be taught explicitly how to think, the Johnsons (1978), Kagan (1992), Slavin (1983), and Bellanca and Fogarty (1991) make the same argument for the social skills of cooperative learning. Explicit instruction is key. As students are taught explicit skills, there must be ways for students to evaluate their progress. The checklist is one such instrument. It provides a quick look at the target skills or behaviors, offers gentle reminders of the expectations and acts as a tool for self-regulatory behavior.

SELF-ADMINISTERED CHECKLISTS

Assessment literature also flags checklists as viable tools for evaluation. In fact, whenever the educational pendulum swings away from letter grades and numerical grade point averages, it swings in the direction of checklists and Likert scales. The checklist, however, when used as a self-evaluation tool, serves as not only an assessment device, but as a reflection of what is important and how students see themselves in relationship to those priority behaviors.

Naturally, not all checklists are records of student behavior or thinking, but all checklists offer the same quick and ready method of reflecting back on something and marking one's opinion accordingly.

Checklists are probably more acceptable as an evaluative, self-assessment tool when accompanied with personal narratives or anecdotes that more fully explain the position marked. The efficiency of the checklist is its hallmark.

How To use checklists in the classroom as self-assessment tools, students must first become familiar with the target items on the list. This can be accomplished in several ways. First, students may simply review the checklist that the teacher prepares or they may actually create an individual checklist to evaluate specific areas that they feel are important.

To illustrate the teacher-made checklists, which often focus on students' procedures or critical elements of an idea, think about a typical lesson or task that can be delineated by guidelines. Then, turn the guidelines into a manageable checklist that students self-administer. For example, a lab experiment checklist might look like this:

LAB CHECKLIST

	Y	N
1. Complete experiment		
2. Return equipment		
3. Incorporate discussion and readings		
4. Complete lab notes		
5. Enter questions		
6. File report		

SELF-ADMINISTERED CHECKLISTS

In this example, the Lab Checklist leads students to reflect on procedures for completing the lab experiment and filing a written report. Each question cues the learner to another part of the total activity.

In the student-generated checklist, students reflect on personal concerns and include these in a checklist form. Even young students can produce a few personal concerns to target for reflection. For example, students may want to use a checklist to evaluate their writing process. They might be concerned with mechanical points, such as a reminder to check spelling or with more esoteric concerns such as, have they read their piece aloud and elicited peer feedback. Either or both of these concerns may appear among other concerns on a student-generated checklist.

WRITING:
FINAL DRAFT CHECKLIST

	Y	N
1. Check spelling.		
2. Read story aloud.		
3. Obtain two peer signatures. (a) (b)		
4. Submit one copy.		
5. File a copy in portfolio.		

Again, checklists do not begin to provide comprehensive self-evaluation, but they do fill a gap that is needed for quick and easy techniques that help students self-evaluate and reflect back on their work. Checklists are short, brief, to-the-point lists that can be checked off even in a momentary reflection. At least it is a reflection!

SELF-ADMINISTERED CHECKLISTS

hen Perhaps one of the first metacognitive tools to use with students is the teacher-made checklist. It is easy, quick, and students know how to use it. Checklists cue students to think about specific things. These cues act as signals for students as they begin to learn about being self-regulatory about their learning. Thus, early in the year, with all grade levels (primary students can use checklists comprised of pictorial symbols), the checklist can be used to introduce the idea of reflective thinking and self-evaluating.

Later on, older students may learn to develop their own checklists as they decide on their own priority concerns. But, always model the use of the checklist. Demonstrate how one reviews the list, thinks about the various elements, and responds. Also, talk about what to do when students find many items on the checklist that they cannot check off because they have not completed them. This awareness leads to changes in behavior in the long run, especially if students begin to see a pattern. For example, if they consistently forget to use spell-check on the word-processing program, this becomes an area to target each time. In fact, students learn as much from the checklist items they can't check off as from the ones they can. The missing checks on the checklist signal a deficit item that needs special attention.

Remember, as students use the checklist, the change in their behavior becomes metacognitive. Encourage both development and reflection with checklists.

One Idea

In order to truly understand the concept of checklists and reflection, have students create their own personal checklists. After students complete a unit in health about fitness and nutrition, ask them to work in cooperative groups to create a concept map of what they have learned relating to fitness and nutrition.

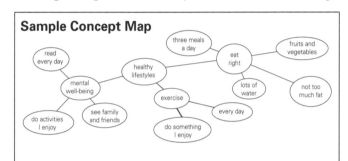

Sample Concept Map

Have them try to answer this question: What does it take to lead a healthy lifestyle? When groups finish their concept maps, allow them to walk from group to group to see what their fellow students included on their maps. Students may re-group and add any ideas to their concept maps that they found helpful.

Next, ask students to draw on the information they learned to create an individual checklist of some realistic behaviors they can follow to lead a healthier life. These can consists of daily habits that they can make part of their routine, such as remembering not to skip breakfast, trying to drink several glasses of water a day, or doing some sort of physical exercise every day. Ask students to use their checklists every day for a week and record and monitor how successfully they follow their lists. After one week, discuss how the checklists are affecting their lifestyles. Ask students to give you an example of how this strategy could apply to other areas and subjects. Challenge them to select and use another application of the checklist strategy and report back to the class how the system is working.

Healthy Lifestyle Checklist

	Y	N
1. Eat 3 meals a day.	✓	
2. Drink 8 glasses of water a day.		✓
3. Exercise every day.	✓	
4. Read every day.	✓	
5. See family and friends every day.	✓	

My Idea

Jot down one idea for this metacognitive tool.

_____

_____

_____

_____

_____

_____

_____

_____

_____

_____

_____

_____

_____

My Reflection

What I Did

Log your use of the idea. Explain what you actually did, giving some details but mostly just the "big idea."

_____

_____

_____

_____

_____

_____

_____

_____

_____

_____

_____

What I Think

Reflect on the activity. What are the pluses and minuses? What other thoughts do you have?

_____

_____

_____

_____

_____

_____

_____

_____

_____

_____

_____

Afterthoughts

STRATEGY 8

What? So What?
Now What?

[STUDENT-LED CONFERENCES]

STUDENT-LED CONFERENCES

**hat** While parent conferences are part of standard evaluation procedures in most schools, student-led conferences are becoming part of the norm. In student-led conferences, the student plays a key role in organizing and executing the conference. The students, following content focus guidelines set by the teacher or the school, gather relevant materials, self-evaluate the materials, and organize individual presentations for their parents.

The ultimate purpose is the same as in the traditional conference: to inform parents of student progress. However, in the student-led conference, the burden of responsibility falls on the students to become reflective and self-evaluative about their work. This does not mean that the teachers do not participate and/or also evaluate student progress, but it does place the onus of concern on the student. Of course, while the students take charge of the conference, the interaction is, in reality, a three-way model, with the teacher, the parents, and the students all participating. However, the students are on focus to metacognitively assess their own growth and development and to share with parents their self-discovered findings.

As student-led conferences take center court in the alternative assessment literature, the metacognitive implications of the strategy are not always stressed. If students are to take on a posture of lifelong learners, they must become acutely aware of their own strengths and weaknesses in order to become self-directed in that learning.

For example, as students review their work for the semester or quarter, refine their portfolios for the presentation to parents, and plot their talk, they automatically must think about and reflect on not only what they have accomplished, but how they have done it. In addition, as they prepare to hold the conference, students reflect on the decisions they are making about the conference, why they have selected to feature certain things, what things to leave out, and what things their parents may want to know that may not have been included. This is the kind of metacognitive reflection that is extremely beneficial for genuine self-evaluation. Also, as students take responsibility for the conference, the shift from teacher-focused communication to a more student-focused conference is readily apparent to all concerned. This is a critical step toward skillful self-assessment. What? So what? Now what? are used to guide that self-reflection.

STUDENT-LED CONFERENCES

 Literature on alternative assessment is ripe with recommendations of student-led conferences and Burke (1993), Ferrara & McTighe (1992), Wiggins (1992), Stiggins (1991), Costa (1991), and Kallick (1992) are among the writers in the field promoting student-led conferences as a viable assessment tool. The strength of the strategy is in the student reflection that is necessary to execute a successful conference. Students must participate fully in order to prepare for the conference and the major component of that preparation is the evaluative "look back" at their own work.

Naturally, the metacognitive processing that results outweighs the time concerns involved in this comprehensive strategy. Just as students become more skilled writers as they start to assess and evaluate their own writing, it follows that students become more skilled learners as they start to assess and evaluate their own learning.

The rationale for self-assessment is overwhelming. For only in self-assessment do students become truly self-regulating. While teachers can provide some guidelines, standards, and benchmarks against which to measure growth, only students themselves can actually attest to real development and progress; only students themselves know where they started compared to where they are now. Self-reporting in student-led conferences opens the door to the inner world of each student.

How To conduct student-led conferences, the most crucial part is helping students prepare for the actual presentation. To do the preparation, the "What? So What? Now What?" question format seems to be a handy guide for students to use because it requires three distinct steps: gathering the materials, processing the relevance, and projecting future application. This is an organizer summary sheet:

STUDENT-LED CONFERENCES

STUDENT-LED CONFERENCES

What?	So What?	Now What?
Topic 1 & artifact	Why it seems important.	How I'll need or use it in the future.
Topic 2 & artifact	Why it seems relevant.	How it connects to other things.
Topic 3 & artifact	Why it seems weak.	How it can be modified.
Topic 4 & artifact	What it represents.	How others might use it.

Each of the three vertical columns are labeled with the key questions: What? So What? Now What? In the "What?" column, students organize various ideas they want to discuss at the conference and identify an accompanying artifact from their portfolio that will help them explain their points. These are listed as topics, but issues, concerns, or focal points serve as well.

In the middle column, "So What?" dictates a processing response that sheds light on why the topic or concern is included. Typical processing statements that students address as they think about the "So What?" column are: Why it (the topic) seems important?; Why it seems relevant?; Why it seems weak or strong? or What it represents?

Finally, the third column, "Now What?", brings the reflection to meaningful application ideas. This is where the students project how the idea (or topic) is useful, connects to other things, can be modified, or perhaps might be of use to others.

While this is only one of many organizers, it seems particularly useful in helping students reflect and prepare for their conference because the three questions proceed from simple information to more personal and more meaningful justification and future application.

An additional column that is sometimes used is labeled, "What else?" This invites spontaneous comments from the students themselves or from the teacher or parents. It rounds out the conference into more of a two- or three-way dialogue rather than a student-led monologue.

STUDENT-LED CONFERENCES

STUDENT-LED CONFERENCE ORGANIZER

What?	So What?	Now What?	What Else?
Topic #1	Reason	Application	Questions or Comments
Topic #2	Reason	Application	Questions or Comments
Topic #3	Reason	Application	Questions or Comments
Topic #4	Reason	Application	Questions or Comments
Topic #5	Reason	Application	Questions or Comments

In any event, the organizer is a vehicle to help students reflect, evaluate, and metacognate about their progress. The conference itself seems to follow pretty smoothly when students have given such thoughtful attention to the preparation. However, they may need further coaching in how to actually conduct the conference, including an explanation of roles, an outline of the time frame, and a discussion of what to expect and what not to expect. All of this leads to the rich metacognitive experience possible when student-led conferences are successfully utilized.

 Prior to the conference and probably ongoing throughout the term, are when the, "What? So What? Now What?" planning takes place for students. Furthermore, do not limit this strategy to older students, for younger students are quite capable of handling the reflective evaluation model described. Of course, their charts are not formally completed in writing, but rather serve as verbal guides to help them organize their information and artifacts.

Also, students may practice leading conferences with their peers prior to actually doing a parent conference. This guided practice helps them gain confidence and develop a sense of timing for the real McCoy.

One footnote seems prudent here. The student-led conference is not an easy strategy to use. Let students become more familiar with the ideas and strategies that promote reflective metacognition before they dive into a full-blown parent conference. Ease into this one.

One Idea

 Since student-led conferences may be a more difficult metacognitive strategy for students to acquire, you may want to offer them more opportunities to practice. In addition to allowing students to practice with their peers, have students invite an older sister or brother or a friend from outside the class to listen to them perform their conference. Ask that the guest offer comments and criticisms to the student so that he or she may improve any weaknesses in using this strategy. If more rehearsal is needed, students can work in cooperative groups. Each student takes a turn at performing the conference and gains advice from group members.

My Idea

Jot down one idea for this metacognitive tool.

_____

_____

_____

_____

_____

_____

_____

_____

_____

_____

_____

_____

_____

My Reflection

What I Did

Log your use of the idea. Explain what you actually did, giving some details but mostly just the "big idea."

_____

_____

_____

_____

_____

_____

_____

_____

_____

_____

_____

_____

What I Think

Reflect on the activity. What are the pluses and minuses? What other thoughts do you have?

_____

_____

_____

_____

_____

_____

_____

_____

_____

_____

_____

_____

Afterthoughts

STRATEGY 9

Storytime!

[ANECDOTES]

ANECDOTES

What Personal anecdotes are the stories students tell about their learning experiences. They are usually narrative renditions of what happened. These are the dinner table conversations that students relate as they relive the episodes from their day in school.

With some prompting, students expound on the events, often beginning at the start of the day and ending with the close of the school day. This long-winded narrative is sometimes referred to as a bed-to-bed story. However, with some gentle prodding, students focus on specific learning episodes and through the telling of these personal vignettes, gain knowledge and insight into their own thinking and learning.

To include the personal anecdote as an evaluation tool implies that there is some reflective analysis of the anecdote. Once related, the skillful listener guides student thinking about the anecdote and steers student reflection toward the metacognitive level of thinking in order to make sense or make meaning of the story.

For example, as a young girl tells a personal anecdote about a field trip to the zoo, she explains that the kids on the bus were predicting all kinds of things about the zoo: what would be the smelliest part, the funniest incident, and the biggest, scariest, and weirdest animal. After listening to her story, her father asks her what prediction she made. At that point, she tells about her prediction that everyone would want to eat lunch as soon as they got off the bus. Then, her father asks her to tell which one was the best prediction and why she thinks so. Of course, she votes for her forecast about wanting lunch. She justifies it as a good prediction because on other trips the same thing always happens. The kids want to eat right away.

This is just a simple example of turning a personal anecdote into a reflective evaluation, but it shows how learnings are inherently embedded in the stories one tells. We learn, implicitly, from the vignettes; however, that learning becomes explicit through reflective questioning. In fact, the stories take on further importance for students as they scrutinize their experience. They think not only about what happens in the story, but how and why it happens.

ANECDOTES

hy Vygotsky (1986) is clear on his stand that learning takes place in the interaction with others; that it is in the relating of ideas and in the exploration of the idea through words that learning happens. According to Vygotsky (1986), as one struggles to encode thoughts into meaningful ideas, that meaning is in turn, constructed in the mind of the learner. His work accentuates the notion that through language and the interactive nature of language, one unveils meaning for oneself.

Students learn as they tell and retell their stories; as they articulate, revise, edit, and exaggerate their anecdotes. It is in the tales we tell that learning takes place. The opportunity to think about a personal experience comes, either in writing or in conversation.

A second part of the rationale for the use of personal anecdotes and vignettes as reflective tools for metacognitive evaluation is Feuerstein's (1980) position on mediation. Without mediation, the story falls down as an evaluative strategy. For it is only when skillful questions are introduced that students are invited into the realm of metacognitive processing.

As in the example of the young girl, the key question at the end of her story really mediated the learning and took it to the reflective phase. Feuerstein (1980) believes that with all learners, mediation strategies trigger more reflective, evaluative thinking, and it is this kind of metacognitive pondering that changes intelligence or modifies the learning capacities of the students.

Both Vygotsky (1986) and Feuerstein (1980) contribute heartily to this theory about mediated language experiences. With this metacognitive tool, students not only relive the experience, but actually reinvent the experience—because in the telling they are learning about themselves; they are moved toward metacognitive awareness and understanding of themselves.

ANECDOTES

w Of all the strategies for reflective thinking, storytelling is by far the easiest to teach students. Children, teens, and young adults are all natural storytellers. Much of their time, between classes and in the formal settings of the classroom, study hall, or school yard is spent telling personal tales about events both in and out of the classroom.

Of course, to formalize this strategy as a metacognitive evaluation technique, teachers must set guidelines, demonstrate, model, and guide students toward more succinct and more purposeful storytelling. With refinement, personal anecdotes can be a favored reflective strategy for both teachers and students. After all, what could be better than to have the teacher encourage students to tell wonderful stories about themselves. It is right up their alley.

Some guidelines that facilitate succinct, purposeful storytelling include two easy-to-remember rules:

RULES FOR ANECDOTES

Rule 1: Tell the best part, not the whole story.

Rule 2: Get to your point; what's the punch line?

Once students learn to think first, select the best part, jump into the story, and then make their point as clearly as possible, the anecdotes become more memorable and more feasible as a classroom evaluation strategy. After some practice in telling short anecdotes with obvious conclusions, students can then learn to be more reflective and evaluative about their stories. They can learn to look behind the story for deeper meanings, for understanding themselves, and for insight into others.

Teachers facilitate this two-part process by first valuing, encouraging, and providing time for the personal anecdotes within the context of the instructional period and second, by guiding the telling and retelling of anecdotes for greater brevity, substance, and reflective evaluation.

ANECDOTES

 Appropriate use of the personal anecdote is usually in pairs because of time constraints. In twos, students easily switch roles of listener and speaker. They are also better able to attend to the interaction because just one other person is in focus—rather than two or three if small groups are used.

Another consideration is to use the personal sharings of anecdotes after students have had some lesson stimulus. Often, teachers notice an energetic hum in the classroom after a stimulating video, story, or science experiment. This signals a time when lots of students are making personal connections; it is a "teachable moment" for storytelling and personal anecdotes.

Then, the teacher takes the necessary time to mediate the experiences and bridge them into big learnings for students. By modeling their reflective stage in whole-class settings, students can then practice with their partners or in smaller groups.

It seems appropriate also, to incorporate storytelling into those wonderfully informal settings in school such as the P.E. class, science lab, outdoor education trip, art class, or during rehearsals for productions or practices for games. In fact, these times of candid interaction actually promote reflective behavior because students are more relaxed and "tuned in" to the experience. Anecdotes become antidotes for many of the more tense, academically focused situations that naturally occur in the classrooms. Reflection can be a handy panacea as well as a catalyst for growth.

One Idea

 Often in elementary grades teachers build in time daily or weekly for journal writing, sharing, show and tell, or other activities in which children can share their thoughts, feelings, and personal experiences and anecdotes. Use these activities as an opportunity to encourage higher-level thinking by prompting students with questions that promote metacognition. Challenge students to explain the hows and whys of their actions and thinking processes whether they are sharing an entry from their journal or discussing something they brought for show and tell.

Encourage other students to ask questions of the speaker that stimulate more reflective thinking. Once the class has observed how the teacher's questioning facilitates metacognition, they will begin to adapt the same techniques. Tape several of the students before trying this strategy and then again after several weeks. Ask the class if they have noticed any difference in the sharing sessions.

> Do they find them more interesting or less interesting?
>
> What kinds of things are they learning about each other?

After discussion, show the tapes of the personal anecdotes, sharing sessions, and show and tells both before and after using metacognition. Talk about how reflecting and discussing topics in depth can be much more interesting and enriching for everyone involved.

My Idea

Jot down one idea for this metacognitive tool.

_____

_____

_____

_____

_____

_____

_____

_____

_____

_____

_____

_____

_____

_____

_____

_____

_____

_____

My Reflection

What I Did

Log your use of the idea. Explain what you actually did, giving some details but mostly just the "big idea."

_____

_____

_____

_____

_____

_____

_____

_____

_____

_____

_____

_____

_____

What I Think

Reflect on the activity. What are the pluses and minuses? What other thoughts do you have?

_____

_____

_____

_____

_____

_____

_____

_____

_____

_____

_____

_____

_____

Afterthoughts

STRATEGY 10

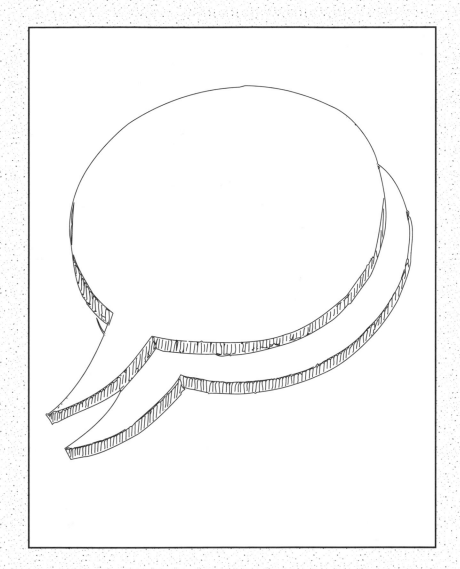

Double-Talk

[DOUBLE-ENTRY JOURNALS]

DOUBLE-ENTRY JOURNALS

What The double-entry journal is a complex log or diary in which two entries are required. The first entry consists of an observation, comment, connection, thought, question, or sketch that occurs to the learner. It is entered systematically whenever the learners choose to record their thoughts and ideas. Some students enjoy writing in their journals daily, while others prefer one or two entries a week. In other cases, the teachers may require a standard number of entries.

However, in a double-entry journal, the initial entry is only half the story. The second part requires an entirely new entry, but this second entry must connect explicitly or implicitly to the first entry. The second entry is often side by side, next to the initial one, and actually extends or enhances the first one. The double entry concept implies that after a first entry, learners revisit the journal, read the entry, and reflect on the words and meaning embedded in the comment. After some genuine reflection and metacognitive evaluation of the entry, students then add a further note or drawing that suggests a more elaborate or detailed observation.

It is speculated that the delayed return to the original journal entry provides the necessary time for valid reflection. In that lapsed time, a sixth sense kicks in and learners are able to extrapolate deeper meaning.

One example of the double-entry journal is with adult learners who are journaling about new teaching strategies to try. Immediately following each teaching episode, they record their thoughts in their journals. They revisit their journals later (at least a day later), read their entries, and write an additional comment. Their journal pages resemble this illustration:

First Thoughts	Afterthoughts
Sept. 20	Sept. 24
Students were unruly about the reports. They were so excited they seemed to make superficial choices.	*In looking over the choices and talking with the kids, their decisions were more thoughtful than first suspected. They seemed to already know the kinds of things that interest them. I have to remember to bring music to the learning.*

DOUBLE-ENTRY JOURNALS

For each entry, another column or spot was reserved along the side, so as the initial entry was read and internalized, the reflection could be written opposite it. In this way, the whole piece was visible at one time.

The comment from the teachers using the double-entry journal reveals an interesting paradox. While none of them comment positively about having to make two entries, most say that it is sometimes startling to see what they had written in the reflection. They are not consciously aware of the insights until they start to write about them. Also, they find themselves writing more in the second entry as they reflect on the meaning behind the initial comments.

The rationale behind the double-entry journal is noted by Jeroski and Brownlie (1992) when they discuss the need for reflective thought in the use of journals. They acknowledge the inherent value in the art of journaling—even without the added benefit of a second look or dual comment. However, they explain that the results of reflective evaluation allow students to see beyond the task or even the feelings that envelop them as they do the task, and into the realm of understanding how and why something happens.

Double-entry journals provide the needed platform for reflective thought if students are to move beyond the "pour and store" model of education and into the realm of reflective or lifelong learning.

While many of us understand the value of letting something be idle for a time before returning to it with fresh eyes and renewed interest, there are not many tools in use in today's schools that actually facilitate that idea. The pacing in most classrooms is too fast and the time too short to foster real reflection and sorely needed time to think over an idea.

However, just as classroom instruction now embraces the idea of writing as a process that takes time and involves first drafts, edits, revisions, and publication, the classroom now seems ready to foster reflection in student work. This is seen in the alternative assessment movement

DOUBLE-ENTRY JOURNALS

in which students are groomed in the portfolio development. As they begin to collect a multitude of artifacts, they learn how to collect, select, reflect, and reject some things. It is this time-consuming reflection that is finally getting some air time in our classrooms. In fact, the double-entry journal demands at least two looks at the same piece: one to observe, synthesize, and record, the other to ponder, reflect, and record.

How

Since many classrooms already incorporate journals as a key tool for metacognitive processing, it is fairly easy to extend the lead to a double-entry journal. To introduce the idea, it is fun to use the analogy of the "double-talk" idea. "Double-talk" in this case means talking to yourself. Students talk to themselves once as they enter some thoughts in their journals. Then, they talk back to themselves as they record their first ideas and comment to themselves about those ideas. In essence, they are talking to themselves and then talking back to themselves. It is pure double-talk.

Let students use the standard journal for a few weeks. Then, incorporate the idea of a second entry, once a week for a few weeks. After students have an opportunity to reflect on their writing and to add to it with some knowing comments, have them evaluate the strategy. Ask students to use a response-in-turn (round robin) approach and respond by saying, "Double-entry journaling is a good idea because _____." Gather the comments on chart paper and suggest that they fill in the blank and add to the list for every journal entry for one month.

After the month is over, evaluate again with the students and draw out the comments that students have about the need for and value of reflective thinking. Continue to monitor double-entry journals and incorporate more opportunities for use as the year goes on.

For younger children, "double-talk" may literally be "double-talk." Instead of writing entries, the teacher may gather initial entries on chart paper and then record the comments from students after they have had a chance to talk with one another about their reflections.

DOUBLE-ENTRY JOURNALS

hen Double-entry journals can be attached to a particular subject area. For example, students may keep a science, math, or literary journal. In any case, these become valuable records of their personal learnings and thoughtful reflections. By infusing journaling and metacognitive evaluation into the reflective second entry, students develop a comprehensive guide to their learnings in that course.

Double-entry journals may be used in a more general sense, detached from any particular subject-matter content. They may simply be used by the student at the end of the day, then at the beginning of the next day, to record and reflect on their learning experiences in general. However, it seems like a wonderful metacognitive extension to the journal to include a double-entry concept.

Also, journals are often used for special occasions such as a middle school trip to Washington, D.C., or on an outdoor education week at a local camp. Much like the travelogue, these targeted journals are also fertile for double-entry activities. In fact, students can make the second entry during the event or they may want to wait until they return. Then, as they reread their entry, they may want to add a metacognitive comment. This model gives the journaling the added flavor that comes with the time lapse. The "double-talk" spans a longer time frame and, thus, is often truly reflective.

In using "double-talk," students are really using a personally targeted self-evaluation tool. It is simple and powerful.

One Idea

You can require middle or high school students to use the double-entry journal technique in a history or government course to have them evaluate historic events or political processes. Ask students to complete a journal entry before each unit of study recording their initial reactions and observations about the subject they are about to study. Two days later, have students reflect on what they had written initially and write a reaction to their writing. Now that they have had time to study the subject and reflect on their initial thoughts, they may expand their journal entries with new insights and opinions. For example, students studying World War II may at first record: "I don't think it was necessary for the United States to become involved in the war. We should have concentrated on our own domestic problems." The second journal entry may read: "I am beginning to understand why the United States became involved. This reminds me of the problem we have today: the decision to send troops to foreign nations to keep peace or transport supplies. I now believe that sometimes, as a world leader, we must become more involved in other countries' affairs." Encourage students to write in their double-entry journals twice a week. From time to time ask students to share their reactions with the class to add personal opinions to the class lectures. As a culminating activity, instead of an exam, ask students to write a paper about their initial reactions to the unit and how the double-entry journal affected their learning.

My Idea

Jot down one idea for this metacognitive tool.

_____

_____

_____

_____

_____

_____

_____

_____

_____

_____

_____

_____

_____

My Reflection

What I Did

Log your use of the idea. Explain what you actually did, giving some details but mostly just the "big idea."

_____

_____

_____

_____

_____

_____

_____

_____

_____

_____

_____

_____

What I Think

Reflect on the activity. What are the pluses and minuses? What other thoughts do you have?

_____

_____

_____

_____

_____

_____

_____

_____

_____

_____

_____

_____

Afterthoughts

IN CLOSING . . .

The purpose of this book, and the activities described thus far, are to show teachers, "how to mediate for metacognitive reflection." As teachers begin to incorporate the ideas into the classroom, students move from tacit use, to aware, strategic and reflective use of metacognition as they plan, monitor and evaluate their work. In essence, they "think about their thinking" and "learn about their learning."

However, to close this book on metacognitive strategies, there is one overriding idea still to address. And that is the idea of the power of self-awareness in changing ourselves. Self-awareness propels one along the learning journey—once we know, we can't *not* know. In the knowing, we can then take action. An illustration of the potential of self-awareness is captured in this simple vignette:

> *A young woman is a guest participant in her friend's yoga class on Saturday morning. Following a wonderful workout of stretching and meditation, the yogi invites the friend to breakfast at a local vegetarian cafe. As the guest proceeds to order, she says, "A cheese omelet with a side of Canadian bacon." Of course, the waitress admonishes her, with, "I'm sorry, we do not serve any meat."*

At this point the guest is a bit embarrassed, laughs nervously at herself and revises her order. But then she turns to her friend and makes a statement reflecting her self-awareness. "I never realized how engrained my habits are . . . and how unaware I am about things like the vegetarian movement. I need to be more sensitive . . . to the current health/fitness scene."

By commenting on herself, the young woman crystallizes not only her awareness of the faux pas, but her self-awareness of her own shortcomings. That metacognitive comment, once expressed, provides an indelible insight into one's self and provides fertile ground for improvement, development and real learning.

While this story serves only as a simple illustration of self-awareness as a tool for change, there is a metacognitive model that seems to provide a similar kind of personal insight. It is referred to as the "Birds of Transfer." The model actually delineates six levels of self-awareness that are associated with the depth of learning or the transfer level of that learning. These six levels of transfer encompass: overlooking, duplicating, replicating, integrating, mapping and innovating. The metaphor of the birds simply provides visual images to accompany the levels. For example, Ollie the Ostrich has his head in the sand and overlooks the possibility of using an idea, while Samantha the Soaring Eagle creatively adapts an idea to the extent that it becomes an innovation in itself.

The chart on the next page (Fogarty, Perkins & Barell, 1992) outlines the six levels with a metaphorical bird paired to each level.

SITUATIONAL DISPOSITIONS FOR TRANSFER

Bird Model	Transfer Disposition	Looks Like	Sounds Like
Ollie the Head-in-the-Sand Ostrich	Overlooks	Persists in writing in manuscript form rather than cursive. (New skill overlooked or avoided.)	*"I get it right on the dittos, but I forget to use punctuation when I write an essay."* (Not applying mechanical learning.)
Dan the Drilling Woodpecker	Duplicates	Plagiarism is the most obvious student artifact of duplication. (Unable to synthesize in own words.)	*"Mine is not to question why—just invert and multiply."* (No understanding of what she/he is doing.)
Laura the Look-Alike Penguin	Replicates	"Bed to bed" or narrative style. "He got up. He did this. He went to bed." or "He was born. He did this. He died." (Student portfolio of work never varies.)	*"Paragraphing means I must have three 'indents' per page."* (Tailors into own story or essay, but paragraphs inappropriately.)
Jonathan Livingston Seagull	Integrates	Incorporates newly learned French words into essay. (Applying: weaving old and new.)	*"I always try to guess (predict) what's going to happen next on T.V. shows."* (Connects to prior knowledge and experience; relates what's learned to personal experience.)
Cathy the Carrier Pigeon	Maps	Graphs information for a social studies report with the help of the math teacher to actually design the graphs. (Connecting to another.)	From a parent: *"Tina suggested we brainstorm our vacation ideas and rank them to help us decide."* (Carries new skills into life situations.)
Samantha the Soaring Eagle	Innovates	After studying flow charts for computer class, student constructs a Rube Goldberg type invention. (Innovates: invents; diverges; goes beyond and creates novel idea.)	*"I took the idea of the Mr. Potato Head and created a mix-and-match grid of ideas for our Earth Day project."* (Generalizes ideas from experience and transfers creatively.)

While "the birds of transfer" provide mental models of the levels of learning and the depth of transfer, it is in the personal application of the models that startling insights occur. It is in the self-awareness of the level of transfer that the learner can then deliberately proceed to a level of more depth.

Again, let's look at personal situations that exemplify each "bird" and how, just in the awareness of level, the learner gains invaluable insight into his or her own development. Since the author assumes that most of the readers are teachers themselves, the illustrations focus on personal teaching episodes or teacher training situations. Each is expressed as a separate vignette.

Ollie
The Head-in-the-Sand Ostrich

(*Overlooks opportunities for transfer*)

Volcanoes and Earthquakes

During an inservice workshop on the "structured overview," a reading strategy to help students understand the science text, the leader passes out a one-page article on volcanoes for participants to use as they practice the strategy.

As the teachers eagerly work with the strategy, they become excited about the information on volcanoes. In fact, they become so immersed in the content, that the strategy inadvertently takes second place in their focus. Just listen to two teachers as they *overlook* the possibilities of using the structured overview and focus, instead, on the topic of volcanoes.

5th Grade Teacher: You're really lucky, Carol. You're studying Hawaii this semester. You can use this great lesson on volcanoes.

6th Grade Teacher: Yeah, you're right. (laughing). Too bad you're doing earthquakes. It won't work for you.

The teachers are so enamored with the idea of volcanoes that they have just experienced, they have forgotten or *overlooked* the strategy of "structuring an overview" or making a concept map as a pre-reading strategy. However, if the instructor reminds them, "Remember, this is about structured overviews. How can you use it?" then transfer could be quite different.

Dan
The Drilling Woodpecker

(Duplicates exactly or copies an idea)

Music to My Ear

Invariably, at some point during every workshop, a participant will stop by the podium and say, "May I have a copy of that?" "I know just where I can use it." Now, this annoys some presenters because they're feeling a bit protective about sharing their workshop material (their bread and butter—so to speak). However, I, on the other hand, am pleased when I hear this request. It signals me that someone has made a critical connection to my content and, in fact, has already targeted a personal application for the material. "May I have a copy of that?" is music to my ears. I welcome the Ditto Dans in my audience because I know they are transferring the learning to a relevant application.

Laura
The Look-Alike Penguin

(Replicates an idea with new uses, but in a similar way)

Teacher!

My story of replicated learning is rooted in the work of Sylvia Ashton Warner, as described in *Teacher*. As a primary teacher, I knew in my heart that the lock-step, basal reader approach to reading was not working. Then I came upon this book in which a dynamic model of teaching was not only described in beautiful detail, but filled with animated photographs of children drawing, writing, reading and dancing. I knew I had happened upon a treasure in Sylvia Ashton Warner's work, *Teacher*.

In my effort to duplicate this rich experience in my own first grade, I scrupulously underlined every key idea in the book, wrote in the column, reread the passages and even cross-referenced it to her first book—a fictional work called *Spinster*. However, in my enthusiasm to copy her methodology, I found gaps in my understanding of what she actually did and subsequently charted my own course—sometimes slightly adrift from her original path and at other times, totally off the beaten path.

In the final analysis, I had not duplicated this New Zealand classroom—because I had some that was hers and some that was mine. On the surface, it was a definite look-alike, but I had really *replicated* the original idea by tailoring the model in my own fashion.

Jonathan Livingston Seagull

(Subtly integrates the new with the old; sometimes not consciously aware of the transfer)

The Weaver

The story I like to tell about the subtle integration of an idea into the classroom involves a high school biology teacher who attended my training in thinking skills. I call him The Weaver, because he is a master at taking an idea and threading it into his existing format. Let me illustrate.

I had spent the better part of one day demonstrating higher-order questions as a thought-provoking strategy for the classroom. Later that week, I visited Brian's biology class and heard this exchange:

"Jose, do you agree or disagree with Watson on this?" (Watson is the author of the biology text.)

"I think I agree with him because his theory matches my experience."

"Good! Now, class, Watson and Jose say . . . ." "Does anyone want to disagree? Can someone give us another view?" and Brian proceeds to weave the higher-order questions and the personal references to his students into his mini-lecture.

I think this is a rich example of integrated transfer; transfer of high-order questions from the workshop in the staff room to subject matter instruction in the classroom. He did not duplicate the workshop activity, but wove the idea into his usual format.

Cathy
The Carrier
Pigeon

(Strategically plots to use the idea in multiple situations)

Real Estate and Gifted Education

The foreign language teacher maps out deliberate applications of newly learned ideas. First, she has her students web the word "France" to see what they know. After this practice of the attribute web with her French I class, she decides to try the same webbing strategy with her adult evening class in which she teaches real estate. She selects "Home Buyer" as her focus words.

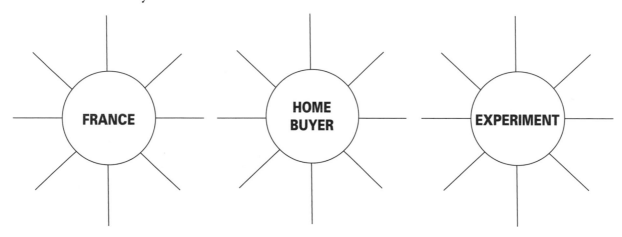

On her drive home that night, her mind is searching and scanning for other uses of this interesting strategy, when she suddenly remembers her upcoming summer school job in which she'll be teaching science to primary-aged children. She makes a mental note to web the word "Experiment" on opening day. And the strategic, planned applications go on as the "mapper" thinks ahead to other uses.

Samantha
The Soaring Eagle

(*Creative, inventive, divergent transfer of an idea*)

The Lucy Jacobs Story

My favorite story of creative transfer involves several other trainers who also conduct workshops on "thinking" in the classroom. Early in my career, I attended a session, in which Lucy Jacobs demonstrated a technique called, The Human Graph.

"Group around me and when I say 'Move,' choose the side you prefer and take your place on that side. Be ready to tell why you're there."

"Ok? Now, would you rather be a mountain climber or a deep-sea diver? Mountain climbers to the right. Deep-sea divers to the left."

The activity was such fun, I immediately incorporated it into my classes, but I changed the idea a bit: *"When I say 'Move,' pick a designated spot, A, B, C, or D, and form a human bar graph. A means slightly agree, B - believe it for myself, C - convince others, and D - die for it. Degrees of disagreement are also A, B, C, or D but on the opposite side. The statement for you to agree or disagree with is:*

"Student rights are infringed upon when there are drug checks of lockers. Now, move."

Years later, Lucy called me and asked for permission to use my human graph strategy. I laughed and said, "Don't you recognize it? I stole this idea from you."

Of course, the idea had been modified to such an extent that Lucy had never connected the two. Now, that's an innovative idea!

Hopefully, these personal anecdotes of the author serve to illustrate the potential of metacognitive insight and self-awareness as self-imposed change agents. But, the true power is only captured by the learners as they examine their own levels of transfer. As they reflect on situations in their own lives in which they exhibit "Ollie" behavior or innovate like a "Sam," learners become privy to insightful thoughts about their own development. It is this self-awareness and the thoughtful articulation about the personal insight that actually create the conditions necessary for change.

To illustrate in a different way the power of self-awareness and thoughtful insight, it is never more obvious than when it is *lacking* in someone. And we all know that individual who captures everyone's attention in an obnoxious display of temper and is totally, profoundly unaware of the impression he or she leaves.

In this example, the learner is oblivious to the impact of his or her actions; in essence, non-reflective and not metacognitive in any way. Of course, it follows that this individual is not likely to change that behavior either, because awareness must precede action. If one is not even aware, then change is not an issue.

However, knowing what we do know about the possibilities for personal growth based on self-awareness and self-knowledge, it behooves the teacher to conduct a personal inventory of the levels of transfer. Take a few minutes to recapture personal learning situations that illustrate the various "birds of transfer."

These anecdotes are invaluable resources as teachers begin their work on metacognitive reflection with students. Once teachers can identify the levels of transfer in themselves, they more readily recognize these levels in their students. Naturally, this is yet another step in the process of mediating skillful metacognitive reflection in the students.

And, once there is an awareness and understanding of one's level of transfer, specific cueing questions can easily guide that transfer to a next level. For example, for each of the six transfers, a thought-provoking question cues further movement.

MAKING CONNECTIONS WITH QUESTIONS

Use bridging questions such as:

Overlooking

Think of an instance when the skill or strategy would be inappropriate.
"I would not use _____ when _____."

Duplicating

Think of an "opportunity passed" when you could have used the skill or strategy.
"I wish I'd known about _____ when _____ because I could've _____."

Replicating

Think of an adjustment that will make your application of _____ more relevant.
"Next time I'm gonna _____."

Integrating

Think of an analogy for the skill or strategy.
"_____ is like _____ because both _____."

Mapping

Think of an upcoming opportunity in classes to use the new idea.
"In _____, I'm gonna use _____ to help _____."

Innovating

Think of an application for a "real-life" setting.
"Outside of school, I could use _____ when _____."

While the "birds of transfer" represent a highly sophisticated metacognitive strategy, as soon as they're introduced, people often sense an "Aha" experience. They gain instant insight into themselves, their peers and colleagues and their students.

These levels of transfer once in our consciousness, seem to provide a magical window for reflection on ourselves and on others. As mentioned earlier, "once we know, we can't not know."

BIBLIOGRAPHY

Anderson, R. C., et al. (1984). *Becoming a nation of readers: The report of the Commission on Reading.* Pittsburgh, PA: National Academy of Education.

Ashton-Warner, S. (1963). *Teacher.* New York: Simon & Schuster.

Ausubel, D. (1978). *Educational psychology: A cognitive view.* (2nd ed.). New York: Holt, Rinehart, & Winston.

Bellanca, J., & Fogarty, R. (1991). (2nd ed., 4th printing). *Blueprints for thinking in the cooperative classroom.* Palatine, IL: IRI/Skylight Publishing, Inc.

Beyer, B. K. (1984, April). Improving thinking skills—a practical approach. *Phi Delta Kappan, 65*(7), 486–490.

Beyer, B. K. (1987). *Practical strategies for the teaching of thinking.* Boston, MA: Allyn & Bacon.

Blanchard, K. H. (1982). *The one-minute manager.* New York: Morrow.

Bloom, B. (1981). *All our children learning.* New York: McGraw-Hill.

Bloom, B. S., Engelhart, M.D., Furst, E.J., Hill, W.H., & Kratwohl, D.R. (1956). *Taxonomy of educational objectives: Cognitive domain, Handbook I.* New York: David McKay Co.

Brown, A. L. (1980). Metacognitive development and reading. In Bruce, B. C., & Brewer, W. F., *Theoretical issues in reading comprehension.* Hillsdale, NJ: Erlbaum.

Brown, A. L. (1978). Knowing when, where and how to remember: A problem of metacognition. In R. Glaser (Ed.), *Advances in instructional psychology.* Hillsdale, NJ: Erlbaum.

Brown, A. L., & DeLoache, J. S. (1980). Skills, plans and self-regulation. In R. S. Siegler (Ed.), *Children's thinking: What develops?* Hillsdale, NJ: Erlbaum.

Brown, A. L., & Palincsar, A. S. (1982). Inducing strategic learning from texts by means of informed, self-control training. *Topics in Learning and Learning Disabilities* 2.

Bruner, J. (1987). Life as narrative. *Social Research, 54,* 11–32.

Bruner, J. (1966). *Toward a theory of instruction.* Cambridge, MA: Belknap Press.

Burke, K. A. (1993). *The mindful school: How to assess thoughtful outcomes.* Palatine, IL: Skylight Publishing, Inc.

Chapman, C. (1993). *If the shoe fits. . . : How to use multiple intelligences in the classroom.* Palatine, IL: IRI/Skylight Publishing, Inc.

Costa, A. L. (1991). *The school as a home for the mind.* Palatine, IL: IRI/Skylight Publishing, Inc.

Costa, A. L. (1984, November). Mediating the metacognitive. *Educational Leadership,* p. 57–62.

Costa, A. L. (1981, October). Teaching for intelligent behavior. *Educational Leadership, 39*(1).

de Bono, E. (1983). The direct teaching of thinking as a skill. *Phi Delta Kappan, 64*(1), 703–708.

de Bono, E. (1976). *Teaching thinking.* New York: Penguin Books.

de Bono, E. (1973). *Lateral thinking: Creativity step by step.* New York: Harper and Row.

Dietz, M. (1993). *Professional development portfolio.* San Ramon, CA: Frameworks.

Eisner, E. W. (1983, October). The kind of schools we need. *Educational Leadership,* 48–55.

Elbow, P. (1981). *Writing with power.* New York: Oxford University Press.

Elbow, P. (1973). *Writing without teachers.* New York: Oxford University Press.

Ferrara, S., & McTighe, J. (1992). Assessment: A thoughtful process. In A. L. Costa, J. Bellanca, & R. Fogarty (Eds.) *If minds matter: A foreword to the future,* vol. II, p. 337–348. Palatine, IL: IRI/Skylight Publishing, Inc.

Feuerstein, R. (1980). *Instrumental enrichment: An intervention program for cognitive modifiability.* In collaboration with Y. Rand, M. B. Hoffman, & R. Miller. Baltimore, MD: University Park Press.

Feuerstein, R., & Feuerstein, S. (1991). Mediated learning experience: A theoretical review. In R. Feuerstein, P. S. Klein, & A. J. Tannenbaum, *Mediated learning experience (MLE): Theoretical, psychological and learning implications.* London: Freund Publishing House.

Flavell, J. H., Friedrichs, A. G., & Hoyt, J. D. (1970). Development changes in memorization processes. *Cognitive Psychology, 1*(4), 324–340.

Fogarty, R. (1991). *The mindful school: How to integrate the curricula.* Palatine, IL: IRI/Skylight Publishing, Inc.

Fogarty, R. (1989). *From training to transfer: The role of creativity in the adult learner.* Doctoral dissertation, Loyola University of Chicago.

Fogarty, R., & Bellanca, J. (1989). *Patterns for thinking—Patterns for transfer.* Palatine, IL: IRI/Skylight Publishing, Inc.

Fogarty, R., & Bellanca, J. (1986). *Teach them thinking.* Palatine, IL: IRI/Skylight Publishing, Inc.

Fogarty, R., & Haack, J. (1986). *The thinking/writing connection.* Palatine, IL: IRI/Skylight Publishing, Inc.

Fogarty, R., Perkins, D., & Barell, J. (1992). *The mindful school: How to teach for transfer.* Palatine, IL: IRI/Skylight Publishing, Inc.

Gardner, H. (1993). *Multiple intelligences: The theory in practice.* New York: Basic Books.

Gardner, H. (1985). *The mind's new science: A history of the cognitive revolution.* New York: Basic Books.

Gardner, H. (1983). *Frames of mind: The theory of multiple intelligences.* New York: Basic Books.

Garfield, C. (1986). *Peak performers: The new heroes of American business.* New York: William Morrow.

Glaser, B. G. (1965). The constant comparative method of qualitative analysis. *Social Problems, 12,* 436-445.

Gordon, W. J. (1961). *Synectics: The development of creative capacity.* New York: Harper & Row.

Guilford, J. P. (1975). *Way beyond I.Q.* Buffalo, NY: Creative Education Foundation.

Holmes, O. W. (1916). *The poet at the breakfast table.* Boston, MA: Houghton Mifflin.

Howard, D. (1994). Pertinence as reflected in personal constructs. *Journal of the American Society for Information Science, 45* (3).

Hunter, M. (1982). *Teaching for transfer.* El Segundo, CA: TIP Publications.

Jeroski, S. (1992). Finding out what we need to know. In A. L. Costa, J. A. Bellanca, & R. Fogarty (Eds.), *If minds matter: A foreword to the future,* vol. II, p. 281-295. Palatine, IL: IRI/Skylight Publishing, Inc.

Jeroski, S., & Brownlie, F. (1992). How do we know we're getting better? In A. L. Costa, J. A. Bellanca, & R. Fogarty (Eds.), *If minds matter: A foreword to the future,* vol. II, p. 321–336. Palatine, IL: IRI/Skylight Publishing, Inc.

Jeroski, S., Brownlie, F., & Kaser, L. (1991). *Reading and responding: Evaluation strategies for teachers.* Scarborough, Ontario: Nelson Canada.

Johnson, D. W., & Johnson, R. (1978). Cooperative, competitive, and individualistic learning. *Journal of Research and Development in Education, 12,* 3–15.

Johnson, D. W., & Johnson, R. (Eds.) (1978). Social interdependence within instruction. *Journal of Research and Development in Education, 12*(1).

Joyce, B., & Showers, B. (1980). Improving inservice training: The message of research. *Educational Leadership, 37*(5), 379–385.

Kagan, S. (1992). *Cooperative learning.* San Juan Capistrano, CA: Resources for Teachers.

Kallick, B. (1992). Evaluation: A collaborative process. In A. L. Costa, J. A. Bellanca, & R. Fogarty (Eds.), *If minds matter: A foreword to the future,* vol. II, p. 313–319. Palatine, IL: IRI/Skylight Publishing, Inc.

Lorayne, H., & Lucas, J. (1974). *The memory book.* New York, NY: Stein & Day.

Marzano, R., & Arredondo, D. E. (1986, May). Restructuring schools through the teaching of thinking skills. *Educational Leadership, 43*(8), 23.

Meeker, M. (1976). *Learning to plan, judge and make decisions.* El Segundo, CA: S.O.I. Institute.

Miles, M. B., & Huberman, A. M. (1984). *Qualitative data analysis: A sourcebook of new methods.* Beverly Hills, CA: Sage.

Ogle, D. (1986). KWL: A teaching model that develops active reading of expository text. *The Reading Teacher, 6,* 564–570.

Palincsar, A. S., & Brown, A. (1984). Reciprocal teaching of comprehension-fostering and comprehension-monitoring activities. *Cognition and Instruction, 1*(2), 117–175.

Parnes, S. (1975). *Aha! Insights into creative behavior.* Buffalo, NY: D.O.K.

Parnes, S. (1972). *Creativity: Unlocking human potential.* Buffalo, NY: D.O.K.

Perkins, D. N. (1989). Are cognitive skills context bound? *Educational Researcher, 18*(1), 16–25.

Perkins, D. N. (1986). *Knowledge as design.* Hillsdale, NJ: Erlbaum.

Perkins, D. N., & Salomon, G. (1988). Teaching for transfer. *Educational Leadership, 46*(1), 22–32.

Peters, T., & Austin, N. (1985). *Passion for excellence.* New York: Random House.

Piaget, J. (1973). *To understand is to invent: The future of education.* New York: Grossman.

Piaget, J. (1972). *The psychology of intelligence.* Totowa, NJ: Littlefield Adams.

Polya, G. (1957). *How to solve it.* Princeton, NJ: Doubleday.

Presseisen, B. Z. (1992). Mediating Learning – The Contributions of Vygotsky and Feuerstein in Theory and Practice. Paper presented at the Annual Meeting of the American Educational Research Association, San Francisco, CA.

Resnick, L. B. (1987). *Education and learning to think.* Washington, DC: National Academy Press.

Resnick, L. B. (1976). *The nature of intelligence.* Hillsdale, NJ: Lawrence Erlbaum.

Rigney, J. W. (1980). Cognitive learning strategies and qualities in information processing. In R. Snow, P. Federico, & W. Montague (Eds.), *Aptitudes, learning, and instruction,* Volume 1. Hillsdale, NJ: Erlbaum.

Senge, P. (1990). *The fifth discipline: The art and practice of the learning organization.* New York: Doubleday.

Slavin, R. E. (1983). *Cooperative learning.* New York: Longman.

Slavin, R. E. (1983). When does cooperative learning increase student achievement? *Psychology Bulletin, 94,* 429–445.

Sternberg, R. J. (1986). *Intelligence applied: Understanding and increasing your intellectual skills.* New York: Harcourt Brace Jovanovich.

Sternberg, R., & Wagner, R. (1982). Understanding intelligence: What's in it for education? Paper submitted to the National Commission on Excellence in Education.

Stiggins, R. J. (1991, March). Assessment literacy. *Phi Delta Kappan,* p. 534–539.

Swartz, R. J. & Perkins, D. N. (1989). Structured teaching for critical thinking and reasoning in standard subject area instruction. Forthcoming in Perkins, Segal, & Voss (Eds.), *Informal reasoning and education.* Hillsdale, NJ: Lawrence Erlbaum Associates.

Taba, H. (1966). *Teaching strategies and cognitive functioning in elementary school children.* (Cooperative Research Project 2404). San Francisco: San Francisco State College.

Thorndike, E. L. (1906) *Principles of teaching.* New York: A.G. Seiler.

Vacca, R. T. (1989). *Content area reading.* Glenview, IL: Scott Foresman.

Vygotsky, L. S. (1986). *Thought and language* (Revised edition). Cambridge, MA: MIT Press.

Wayman, J. (1980). *The other side of reading: The forgotten skill.* Carthage, IL: Good Apple, Inc.

Whimbey, A. (1975). *Intelligence can be taught.* New York: Innovative Science.

Whimbey, A., & Lochhead, J. (1984). *Beyond problem solving and comprehension* (3rd ed.). Philadelphia: Franklin Institute Press.

Whimbey, A., & Lochhead, J. (1982). *Problem solving and comprehension* (3rd ed.). Philadelphia: Franklin Institute Press.

White, R. T. (1993, April). Insights on conceptual change derived from extensive attempts to promote metacognition. Paper given at the meeting of the American Educational Research Association, Atlanta, GA.

White, R. T., & Gunstone, R. (1992). *Probing understanding.* London: Falmer.

Wiggins, G. (1992, May). Creating tests worth taking. *Educational Leadership,* p. 26–33.

Williams, R. B. (1993). *More than 50 ways to build team consensus.* Palatine, IL: IRI/Skylight Publishing, Inc.

Wittrock, M. C. (1967). Replacement and nonreplacement strategies in children's problem solving. *Journal of Educational Psychology,* 69–74.

INDEX

ACE technique, 22
Actualization of the goal, 56
AGO (Aims, Goals and Objectives), 141
Alarm clock, 111-20
Anderson, R. C., 6, 7, 47
Anecdotes, 271-80
Anticipation, 38
Art, using inferences with works of, 50
Ashton-Warner, Sylvia, 297
Attribute web, 299
Audiotape, in conferencing strategy, 160
Austin, Nancy, 65
Ausubel, D., 39, 80
Awareness in metacognition, xv

Barell, J., 105, 169, 214, 215, 233, 292
Behaviors
     in enhancing metacognition, xiv
     labeling students', xiv
Bellanca, J., 15, 31, 33, 141, 159, 204, 253
Benchmarks, 64, 66
BET strategy, 38, 140
Beyer, B. K., xv, 150, 253
Bias, 14
Big idea, 241-50
Birds of Transfer, 292-300
Blanchard, K. H., 56
Bloom, B., 30, 31, 95, 213, 215
Body language, making inferences about, 46
Bo Peep theory of transfer, 170
Brainstorming
     in bridging strategy, 172
     in connecting elephants strategy, 236
     in generalizing strategy, 244
     in KWL strategy, 81

in prompting strategy, 150
in strategic planning, 67
in tape recording strategy, 125
in "What-if" problem solving, 75
Bridging strategy, 167-76
Brown, A. L., x, 39, 112
Brownlie, F., 283
Bruner, J., 242
Burke, K. A., 223, 263

Camus, Albert, vii
Carlyle, Thomas, 87
Cathy the Carrier Pigeon model, 293, 299
Cause and effect circles, 80
Chart story, 134
Checklists, self-administered, 251-60
Checkmate, 251-60
Choose your spot, 201-10
Choosing, in enhancing metacognition, xiii
Chunking, 66
Class field trip, planning a, 67
Classification, 107
Concept attainment, 242
Concept map, 24, 80, 257, 295
Conferences, student-led, 261-70
Conferencing strategy, 157-66
Connecting elephants strategy, 231-40
Constructivist theory of learning, 7, 47
Cooperative learning, xvii, xviii-xix
CoRT thinking resources, 193
Costa, Art, xi, xii, xx, 95, 188, 224, 263,
Creative transfer, 300
Credit, taking, in enhancing metacognition, xiii
Cue cards, 149-56
Cueing technique, to prompt metacognition, xv

Dan the Drilling Woodpecker model, 293, 296
de Bono, E., 74, 141, 192, 193
Dietz, M., 223
Double-entry journals, 281-90
Double-talk, 281-90
Dramatization, in enhancing metacognition, xiv
Drawings, 116
Duplication, 296, 302

Eisner, E. W., 179
Elbow, Peter, 15
Evaluating strategies, ix-x, 107, 188
    anecdotes, 271-80
    double-entry journals, 281-90
    evaluating, 211-20
    generalizing, 241-50
    How can I use this?, 231-40
    human graph, 201-10
    PMI, 191-200
    portfolio registry, 221-30
    self-administered checklists, 251-60
    student-led conferences, 261-70
Extrapolating, 38

Facial expressions, making inferences about, 46
Fat questions, 29-36
Ferrara, S., 222, 263
Feuerstein, R., x, 123, 151, 273
Film footage, 21-28
Films, and use of prediction, 40
Fishbone diagram, 80
Fisher, Leonard Everett, 50
Flavell, John, x
Flowcharts, 80
Focused learning, 8
Fogarty, R., 15, 31, 33, 105, 141, 159, 169, 204, 214,
    215, 233, 253, 292
Forecasting, 38
Foreign language instruction, 299

Gardner, Howard, 24
Garfield, C., 56
Generalizing strategy, 107, 241-50
Gifted education, 299
Glaser, B. G., 133, 179-80
Goal post strategy, 55-62
Goal-setting strategy, 55-62
    prediction skills in, 39
Good Shepherd theory, 170
Gordon, W. J., 205
Graphic organizers, xix, 24
Guessing, 38
Guided reflection, 16
Guilford, J. P., 141

Higher-order questions, 29-36
History, observation techniques in, 182
Holmes, Oliver Wendell, 31

Homer, Winslow, 50
Howard, D., 113
How can I use this?, 231-40
Huberman, A. M., 132, 179
Human graph, 201-10
Hunter, Madeline, 180
Hypothesizing, 38

I can't, outlawing, in enhancing metacognition, xiii
Inferences
    distinguishing between observation and, 48-49
    making, 38, 45-54, 107
Inking your thinking, 13-20
Innovation transfer disposition, 293, 300, 302
Instant replay technique, 121-30
Integration transfer disposition, 293, 298, 302
Inventing, 107

Jeroski, S., 283
Johnson, D. W., 159
Johnson, Nancy, 204, 253
Johnson, R., 159
Jonathan Livingston Seagull model, 293, 298
Journals. See also Learning logs
    double-entry, 281-90
    in elementary grades, 276
    in enhancing metacognition, xiv
    KWL strategy in, 82
    stem statements in, 8
Joyce, B., 142

Kagan, S., 159, 253
Kallick, B., 263
KWL strategy, 79-86, 141

Labeling
    strategy of, 103-10
    and use of fat and skinny questions, 32
Language arts, graphic representations in, 24
Lateral thinking, 193
Laura the Look-Alike Penguin model, 293, 297
Lead-in statements, 15
Learning logs, 13-20. See also Journals
Likert scales, 254
Lincoln, Abraham, 1
Lockhead, J., 95
Lorayne, Harry, 22, 141

Mapping transfer disposition, 293, 299, 302
Mathematics
    recovery strategies in, 114
    think-aloud strategies in, 97, 98
Matrix model, 65, 80
McTighe, J., 222, 263
Mediated log entry, 15
Meeker, M., 141
Memoing strategy, 131-38
Memory, role of visualization in, 22-23

Mental menus, 139-48
Mental seesaw model, 73
Metacognition
    cueing technique to prompt, xv
    definition of, vii, viii
    direct instruction in, xii
    elements in, x
    evaluating, ix-x, 187-289
    experts on, x-xi
    infusing instruction in, xii
    levels of, xv
    monitoring in, ix, 87-185
    planning in, viii, 1-86
    reasons for teaching, xvi-xvii
    strategies for enhancing, xii-xvi
    and the teacher, xvii-xix
Metacognitive mirrors, xx-xxi
Metacognitive reflection, xx
Microscope, 177-86
Miles, M. B., 132, 179
Mnemonic devices, 140
Modeling
    in enhancing metacognition, xiv
    and use of fat and skinny questions, 32
Monitoring strategies, ix, 88-89
    bridging, 167-76
    conferencing, 157-66
    labeling behaviors, 103-10
    memoing, 139-48
    prompting, 149-56
    recorded observations, 177-86
    recovery strategies, 111-20
    self, xi-xiii
    tape recordings, 121-30
    think aloud, 93-102
Mrs. Potter's Questions, 211-20
Multimedia classroom, use of prediction in the, 40
Multiple criteria, evaluating with, in enhancing
    metacognition, xiii

Observations
    distinguishing between inferences and, 48-49
    recorded, 177-86
Ogle, Donna, 80
Ollie the Head-in-the-Sand Ostrich model, 295, 293
OPV (Other Point of View), 141, 193
Outlawing "I Can't", in enhancing metacognition, xiii
Overlooking transfer disposition, 293, 295, 302

Palincsar, A. S., x
Paraphrasing, in enhancing metacognition, xiii
Parnes, S., 73, 233, 235
Perkins, D., xv, 105, 113, 151, 169, 170, 214, 215, 233, 234, 292
Peters, Tom, 65
Physical education
    graphic representations in, 24
    visualization as planning strategy in, 25

Piaget, Jean, 242
Pie in the face, 45-54
Plagiarism, 293
Plan, distinguishing between strategic plan and, 64
Planning strategies, viii, xii-xiii, 3
    goal setting, 55-62
    higher-order questions, 29-36
    KWL, 79-86
    learning logs, 13-20
    making inferences, 45-54
    predicting, 37-44
    strategic planning, 63-70
    thoughtful lead-ins, 5-12
    visualization, 21-28
    "What-if" problem solving, 71-78
PMI strategy, 74, 141, 191-200
Polya, G., 73
Portfolio registry strategy, 221-30
Possibility thinking, 141
Post-it notes, 131-38
Predicting strategy, 37-44, 107
Pre-learning prompts, 14
Prime the pump, 79-86
Prior knowledge
    in KWL strategy, 81, 83
    in prediction strategy, 39
    in recorded observation strategy, 181
    and stem statements, 6
Problem solving, 107
    "What-if," 71-78
Prompting strategy, 149-56

Questions
    generating, in enhancing metacognition, xiii
    higher-order, 29-36
    Mrs. Potter's, 211-20
    reflective, 212

Reading
    comprehension in, 7, 16
    as constructive process, 38
    research on metacognition in, 6-7
    strategies in, viii
    structured overview in, 295
    think-aloud strategies in, 97
Recorded observations, 177-86
Recovery strategies, 111-20
Reflecting back students' ideas, in enhancing
    metacognition, xiii
Reflective evaluation, xxi
Reflective monitoring, xx
Reflective questions, 212
Reflective stage of metacognition, xvi
Replication transfer disposition, 293, 297, 302
Response-in-turn approach, 284
Revolving Door, 221-30
Rigney, J. W., xi
Road map, 63-70

Role playing
in conferencing strategy, 159
in connecting elephant strategy, 234
in enhancing metacognition, xiv
in labeling behavior, 107
Roll the dice, 37-44
Rote memory, x
Round robin idea, 8, 284

Salomon, G., 169, 234
Samantha the Soaring Eagle model, 293, 300
Scaffolding, 39, 235
Schemata, 38
Science
graphic representations in, 24
recovery strategies in, 114
Seesaw thinking, 71-78
Self-administered checklists, 251-60
Self-awareness, 291-92
and situational dispositions for transfer, 293-300
Self-directed learning model, learning logs in, 15
Self-evaluation, connecting elephant strategy in, 232
Self-monitoring, xi-xiii
Senge, Peter, 65
Sharing, 276
Show and tell, 276
Showers, B., 142
Situational dispositions for transfer, 293-94
"Six hats" strategies, 193
Skinny questions, 29-36
Slavin, R. E., 159, 253
Small group work, xvii
Social studies
double-entry journal technique in, 286
graphic representations in, 24
Sociology, observation techniques in, 182
Soup cans, 103-10
Staged conferencing simulations, 159
Stem statements, 5-12
Sternberg, R., xii
Stiggins, R. J., 263
Storytime, 271-80
Strategic planning, 63-70
Strategic use of metacognition, xv-xvi
Structured overview, 295
Structure of the intellect (SOI) model, 141
Student-led conferences, 261-70
Student reflection, xvii
Students' terminology, clarifying, in enhancing
metacognition, xiv
Student thinking, levels of, 31
Swartz, R. J., xv, 113
Synectics model, 205

Taba, H., 242
Tacit use, of metacognition, xv
Talk to yourself, 93-102
Tape recording, 121-30
and use of prediction, 40
T-chart, in distinguishing between skinny and fat
questions, 33
Teachers, and metacognition, vii-xix
Teacher-questioning techniques, transfer talk in, 169
Technology, think-aloud strategies in, 97
Think-aloud strategy, 93-102
Thinking, effect of stem statements in, 6
Thoughtful lead-in strategy, 5-12
Thoughtfulness, and teaching, xviii-xix
Three-story intellect, 31
Thumbs up/thumbs down, 191-200
"To-do" list, 57
Touch Down, P.F.C., 142-43
Tracking, 139-48
Transfer, metacognitive model of, 291-302
Transfer of learning, connecting elephant strategy in, 232
Transfer talk, 167-76
Two-way talk, 157-66

Vacca, R. T., 80
Venn diagram, 24, 80
Videos
in conferencing strategy, 160
and use of prediction, 40
Visualization, 21-28
Visual organizer, in mental problem solving, 73
Visual/spatial intelligence, 24
Vocabulary, recovery strategies in learning, 116
Vygotsky, L. S., 105, 273

Wagner, R., xii
Warner, L. S., 297
Wayman, Joe, 22
Web, 80
attribute, 299
concept, 24, 80, 257, 295
"What-if" problem solving, 71-78
"What if?/Yes, but . . ." seesaw model, 73–75
What? So What? Now What?, 261-70
Whimbey, A., xii, 95
Wiggins, G., 263
Williams, Bruce, 65
Wonder, John, 187
Wraparound strategy, 8
Writing process
acronym for, 142
conferencing in, 158
think-aloud strategies in, 97

IRI SkyLight
EDUCATIONAL TRAINING AND PUBLISHING

LEARN FROM OUR BOOKS
<u>AND</u> FROM OUR AUTHORS!
Bring Our Author-Trainers To Your District

Now that you have benefited from IRI/Skylight's high-quality publications, extend your learning by meeting the actual authors. IRI/Skylight authors are seasoned professionals with a wealth of knowledge and experience. They offer dynamic, exciting presentations. Many authors are available to visit your site and discuss their particular areas of expertise!

Training of Trainers

IRI/Skylight provides comprehensive inservice training for experienced educators who are qualified to train other staff members. IRI/Skylight presenters possess years of experience at all levels of education and include authors, field experts, and administrators. IRI/Skylight's training of trainers program is the most powerful and cost-effective way to build the skills of your entire staff.

Training Programs

IRI/Skylight training is available in your district or intermediate agency. Gain practical techniques and strategies for implementing the latest findings from educational research. No matter the topic, IRI/Skylight has an experienced consultant who can design and specially tailor an inservice to meet the needs of your school or organization.

Network

An IRI/Phi Delta Kappa partnership, *The Network of Mindful Schools* is a program of site-based systemic change, built on the core values advocated by Arthur L. Costa. Each member school is committed to restructuring itself to become a "home for the mind." The network is built on three elements: a site leader, a faculty that functions as a team, and an external support system to aid in school transformation.

To receive a free copy of the IRI/Skylight Catalog, find out more about The Network of Mindful Schools, or for more information about trainings offered by IRI/Skylight, contact:

IRI/Skylight Publishing, Inc.
200 E. Wood Street, Suite 274, Palatine, Illinois 60067
800-348-4474
FAX 708-991-6420

There are
one-story intellects,
two-story intellects, and three-story
intellects with skylights. All fact collectors, who have
no aim beyond their facts, are one-story men. Two-story men
compare, reason, generalize, using the labors of the fact
collectors as well as their own. Three-story men
idealize, imagine, predict—their best
illumination comes from above,
through the skylight.
—*Oliver Wendell*
Holmes